VARIANT LIFESTYLES AND RELATIONSHIPS

FAMILY STUDIES TEXT SERIES

Series Editor: RICHARD J. GELLES, *University of Rhode Island*
Series Associate Editor: ALEXA A. ALBERT, *University of Rhode Island*

This series of textbooks is designed to examine topics relevant to a broad view of family studies. The series is aimed primarily at undergraduate students of family sociology and family relations, among others. Individual volumes will be useful to students in psychology, home economics, counseling, human services, social work, and other related fields. Core texts in the series cover such subjects as theory and conceptual design, research methods, family history, cross-cultural perspectives, and life course analysis. Other texts will cover traditional topics, such as dating and mate selection, parenthood, divorce and remarriage, and family power. Topics that have been receiving more recent public attention will also be dealt with, including family violence, later life families, and fatherhood.

Because of their wide range and coverage, Family Studies Texts can be used singly or collectively to supplement a standard text or to replace one. These books will be of interest to both students and professionals in a variety of disciplines.

Volumes in this series:

1. LATER LIFE FAMILIES, Timothy H. Brubaker
2. INTIMATE VIOLENCE IN FAMILIES,
   Richard J. Gelles & Claire Pedrick Cornell
3. BECOMING A PARENT, Ralph LaRossa
4. FAMILY RESEARCH METHODS, Brent C. Miller
5. PATHS TO MARRIAGE, Bernard I. Murstein
6. WORK AND FAMILY LIFE, Patricia Voydanoff
7. REMARRIAGE, Marilyn Ihinger-Tallman & Kay Pasley
8. FAMILY STRESS MANAGEMENT, Pauline Boss
9. DIVORCE, Sharon J. Price & Patrick C. McKenry
10. FAMILIES AND HEALTH, William J. Doherty & Thomas L. Campbell
11. VARIANT LIFESTYLES AND RELATIONSHIPS,
    Bram P. Buunk & Barry van Driel

Bram P. Buunk
and
Barry van Driel

VARIANT
LIFESTYLES
AND
RELATIONSHIPS

FAMILY STUDIES
TEXT SERIES 11

SAGE PUBLICATIONS
The International Professional Publishers
Newbury Park   London   New Delhi

For information address:

SAGE Publications, Inc.
2455 Teller Road
Newbury Park, California 91320

SAGE Publications Ltd.
6 Bonhill Street
London EC2A 4PU
United Kingdom

SAGE Publications India Pvt. Ltd.
M-32 Market
Greater Kailash I
New Delhi 110 048 India

Printed in the United States of America

Library of Congress Cataloging-in-Publication Data

Buunk, Bram.
    Variant lifestyles and relationships / Bram P. Buunk & Barry van Driel.
        p. cm. — (Family studies text series ; v. 11)
    Bibliography: p.
    Includes index.
    ISBN 0-8039-3059-3. — ISBN 0-8039-3060-7 (pbk.)
    1. Sex customs — United States. 2. Social structure—United States. 3. Life style.   I. Driel, Barry van. II. Title.
III. Series.
HQ18.U5B88   1989
306.7—dc

1989-4309
CIP

SECOND PRINTING, 1991

Contents

Foreword

In this book we present an overview of what the social and behavioral sciences have taught us, mainly in the past two decades, about variant lifestyles and relationships. Although we use historical and ethnographic material to illustrate, amongst others, that variant lifestyles are not as new as often is supposed, our main focus is upon empirical findings from sociology, and from social psychology, a discipline in which the interest for intimate relationships has grown considerably during the past decade.

We have written this book primarily for undergraduates enrolled in courses on close relationships, family studies and human sexuality, though graduate students and interested laypersons will also find the information presented in this book to be a valuable tool in comprehending the major issues involved in variant lifestyles. The chapters have been written in such a way as to stimulate discussion. For this reason, questions and assignments have been added at the end of each chapter. To enhance the readability of the book, a limited number of references has been included in each chapter, with an emphasis on recent studies. To make the book accessible to a wider audience, we have also deliberately steered away from professional jargon and complicated statistical issues as much as possible. Although the book is meant to be read as a whole, and it is structured for this purpose, each individual chapter can be read separately.

Working on this book has been a pleasure for both of us, not in the least because a number of individuals have helped us in various ways. First of all, we want to express our appreciation to Lea de Haan-Wagner, Jolanda Ariens, and Nettie Theyse, who typed with much patience the numerous versions of this manuscript. Furthermore, we would like to thank the series editors Richard Gelles and Alexa Albert, as well as the anonymous reviewers for their constructive criticism and valuable remarks. Thanks are also due to Lea Shamgar-Handelman of the Hebrew University in Jerusalem, who made it possible for the first author to spend two months as a visiting scholar at this university to work on this book. Last but not least, we are indebted to Hedy Kleijweg and

Frieda Vreeman van Driel, not only for their patience and support, but also for their professional advice and criticism. We would especially like to thank Hedy Kleijweg for her editing contribution.

— Bram P. Buunk
— Barry van Driel
Nijmegen, The Netherlands
Hod Ha Sharon, Israel
Santa Cruz, California

CHAPTER 1

Marriage, Family, and Variant Lifestyles: Persistence and Change

MARRIAGE: CRITICISM AND ALTERNATIVES

FOR AT LEAST A CENTURY, American observers have warned against the negative consequences of changes in family life, such as the rising divorce rate and the declining birth rate. Concern has mounted in the past few decades as both conservatives and liberals have expressed their doubts about current developments. It has even been suggested that the institutions of marriage and the family are facing a serious crisis, a situation that is deplored by most observers. We are frequently confronted with references to a variety of degenerative symptoms that point to the decline of the institutions of marriage and the family: the isolation of the nuclear family, the skyrocketing divorce rate, the widening generation gap, the loss of parental authority, the general dissatisfaction with marriage, the increase in extramarital sex, the lack of commitment as manifested in the increasing rates of nonmarital cohabitation, the egotism of those electing to voluntarily forsake children, and the negative effects of maternal employment (Caplow et al., 1982). It has also been argued that the intrusion of the government and outside agencies into the protective shell of the family system has destroyed opportunities for a warm interpersonal environment with high levels of commitment to one another. Keniston (1960), a long time observer of American youth and the American family, has argued on several occasions that the integrity of the American family is being threatened by the usurpation of family functions and family authority by other social institutions, such as the schools, the medical profession, the courts, social welfare agencies, social scientists, and psychologists. Recently, the rapid spread of the deadly disease AIDS has been seen by many observers as the latest proof of the disastrous consequences of the erosion of traditional values of commitment and sexual monogamy.

The idea that marriage and the family are facing a serious crisis is an inaccurate, though understandable, appraisal of the current state of

affairs. In fact, increased affluence, increasing equality between husband and wife, as well as the much better methods for contraception
today, have made the opportunities for an intimate, companionate,
satisfactory marital relationship perhaps better than ever before. Yet the
very same factors have brought about significant changes in American
marriage and family life over the past two decades, changes that appear
to indicate a diminished interest in marriage and family life as it was
traditionally envisioned. The first signs of these changes manifested
themselves toward the end of the 1960s, when a variety of so-called
"alternative lifestyles" garnered considerable public attention. At a time
when AIDS was completely unheard of, reports appeared in the media
about "hippie" communes where drugs were widely used and free love
was practiced, "swinging" couples that engaged in group sex and orgies,
"open marriages" where spouses gave one another the freedom to
engage in extramarital affairs, student couples who started living together on or off campus without first getting married, and singles who
engaged in a promiscuous lifestyle and did not seem at all eager to
marry. Perhaps most shocking to the American public were gays who
first admitted and then defended their lifestyle in public, and women
who gave up their heterosexual identity and became lesbian as part of
their liberation from male oppression.

Most of these lifestyles arose from the counterculture of the sixties,
a period of seemingly rapid social change, in which, for the first time,
the foundations of American society and the conventional wisdom of
prior generations were being seriously questioned (Bellah, 1976). The
legitimacy of America's cherished institutions was in danger and widespread protest arose against their being presumed obsolete. This protest
thus constituted a challenge to traditional American values, and most
of the alternative lifestyles that became so visible toward the end of the
sixties were, to a large degree, an attempt to live out a value pattern
different from mainstream society. This alternative value pattern included the cultivation of feeling over mind; an orientation on the
present instead of on the future; an egalitarian versus a conventional
role pattern; a strong emphasis upon openness, honesty, and intimacy;
a repudiation of materialism; a search for spirituality; and an emphasis
on play instead of work and ambition. Those involved in the "new"
lifestyles were trying to escape what they saw as the confines of the
affluent middle class family with its emphasis upon hard work, delayed
gratification, occupational mobility, and materialistic consumption.
Instead, self-actualization, autonomy, and warm interpersonal relations
were accentuated. Within this world view, the traditional nuclear family

was viewed as an obsolete institution that was very much at odds with such values (Cogswell, 1975).

Members of the counterculture and other young people rebelling against society were not the only ones who were critical of traditional marriage and family life. Some members of the scientific community also held these views. Towards the end of the sixties and at the beginning of the seventies, several social scientists published elaborate critiques of traditional marriage and family, emphasizing the negative consequences of the traditional lifestyles for the individuals immersed in them. For example, according to Ray Birdwhistell (1970), the American model of marriage and family has so many idealized objectives to pursue that a given couple is extremely likely to fail in accomplishing them. The model idealizes the closed, exclusive, and isolating dyad, asserting that the spouses should fulfill *all* of the other's emotional and physical needs. It views the parents as being not only morally and legally responsible for their children, but responsible for the personalities of their offspring as well. The American family, according to Birdwhistell, is an institution that demands too much, with unattainable goals that leave people failing both as spouses and parents. Other social scientists criticized the monogamous character of traditional marriage. Thus, Smith and Smith (1974, p. 35), in an introduction to a collection of research and theoretical papers on nonmonogamous arrangements, described monogamous marriage as ". . . in its own macabre way, a legitimate form of emotional and erotic bondage, as evidenced by its obligatory character." According to these authors, the monogamic code is antisocial and contrary to human nature. They pointed to the increasing opportunity for, and prevalence of, many types of extramarital relationships. Still others particularly focused upon the male dominance and female subordination in traditional marriage, and the concomitant unequal division of tasks and responsibilities that, according to some social scientists, made women, once they married ". . . invariably disappointed and often unhappy" (Perrucci and Targ, 1974, p. 15).

Criticism of the institutions of marriage and the family, as well as the existence of "alternative lifestyles," is, however, nothing new. Since the last century, a more or less coherent set of objections to traditional marriage and the family, as well as proposals for change, has been voiced. They played, albeit in different versions, a role in such diverse situations as the experiments after the Russian Revolution, the beginning stages of the Israeli kibbutzim, and a number of radical communes that emerged in the United States and Western Europe during the nineteenth century. Such experiments were influenced by radical social criticism originating from Marxism, humanism, and feminism. Some issues have been rather constant in this critical thinking about marriage and the family, though they have different emphases that are related to time and circumstance.

1) Gender roles. A critique of traditional marriage and family life as fostering male supremacy, and a desire to promote the entrance of women into the work force, as well as gender role equality at home.

2) Pair relationships. The condemnation of private, exclusive, and even permanent relationships, which are viewed as an undesirable limitation of one's possibilities for love, and as fostering egotistical tendencies and weakening the motivation to be involved in, or work for, the community as a whole.

3) Legalization. Opposition to marriage as a legal institution due to its legitimation of the inferior position of women, coupled with the idea that relationships should be freely chosen between autonomous individuals and not legally constrained in an artificial way.

Although such ideas have been voiced primarily since the last century, aversion to marriage, as well as the existence of alternative lifestyles, dates back to much earlier periods. For example, the apostle Paul saw celibacy as the preferred state, although it was, in Paul's famous words, "better to marry than to burn." Marriage has not always been held in high esteem in Western Europe as it was often a business transaction: it took the form of a private contract (between two families or individuals) that, in the early Middle Ages, usually was not enforced through a church ceremony. Longings for intimacy were often expressed outside the conjugal union. Until the eleventh century, divorce was easy to obtain in England and many individuals (including numerous clergymen) cohabited without the sanctity of marriage. And centuries later, in 1799, *The Lady's Magazine* complained that

> "Railing at matrimony is become so fashionable a topic that one can scarcely step into a coffeehouse or tavern but one hears declamations against being clogged with a wife and a family, and a fixed resolution of living a life of liberty, gallantry, and pleasure, as it is called" [sic] (Stone, 1977, p. 242).

The existence of extramarital affairs has been noted throughout history. Often such affairs had a strong overtone of love and involvement, especially when marriage was seen as a business transaction. Among the nobility, these affairs were often tolerated and even encouraged. Involuntary and voluntary singlehood are not, of course, modern inventions. At many points in time there have been those who felt it was better to be celibate if one wanted to devote oneself to goals such as art, religion, or science. Furthermore, until the beginning of this century, many younger sons of farmers, nobility, and gentry in Western Europe remained unmarried as there was not enough property to divide among all of the sons. Finally, communal arrangements can be found throughout history. The early Christians lived in communal (though not at all promiscuous) groups, and the same can be said of monks who resided — and still do so — together in monasteries. Of course, the motivations behind, as well as the specific forms of, alternative lifestyles in the past were quite often different from today (Murstein, 1974).

IMPACT UPON SOCIETY

Although the "alternative lifestyles" that arose out of the 1960s counterculture were by no means a modern phenomenon, they were a sign of important changes that would affect the institutions of marriage and family (Macklin, 1987). Social scientists sensed that such changes were underway and started conducting research on the various lifestyles that were making headlines by the end of the sixties. Probably the first scholarly — though not very research-oriented — review in this area was a special issue published by the journal *The Family Coordinator,* edited by Marvin Sussmann, in 1972. This issue contained articles on, among others, communes, comparisons between conventional and counterculture families, open marriage, cohabitation, group marriage, and lesbian relationships — a list of topics that closely corresponds to the content of this book, with the exception of singlehood, which did not become visible as an alternative lifestyle until several years later (Stein, 1975). All contributors to this special alternative lifestyle issue felt that the institution of marriage was in bad shape, barely managing to survive in a sick society. There was general agreement that serious changes in the marital institution were necessary, or were already nascent. In this same issue, George and Nena O'Neill (1972) proposed, as an alternative to traditional marriage, the concept of the "open marriage," characterized by such guidelines as living for the present, realistic expectations, privacy, role flexibility, open and honest communication, open companionship, equality, identity, and trust. In 1975, *The Family Coordinator* published a follow-up of the 1972 issue, and in the intervening years several edited volumes on alternative lifestyles appeared (e.g., Smith and Smith, 1974; Libby and Whitehurst, 1973). The impact of non-traditional family forms on social science became especially obvious when a special chapter was devoted to this topic by the prominent *Journal of Marriage and the Family,* in a review of a decade of research on the theme of the family (Macklin, 1980). And the recent, prestigious *Handbook of Marriage and the Family* contains an extensive chapter on this subject (Macklin, 1987).

Although not always recognized, mainstream society was, indeed, significantly affected by the values and lifestyles that arose from the counterculture of the sixties, but the impact was different from what many had initially hoped or feared. Daniel Yankelovich (1982), the well-known investigator of social trends, was struck by the fact that in the sixties, a time when American society *appeared* to change dramatically (the time of the anti-Vietnam War protests, flower-power, communes, love-ins, and the sexual revolution), the large majority of Americans seemed completely untouched. However, it was during the less revolutionary seventies, when the media were retreating from liberal social attitudes, that startling cultural changes *did take* place. According to Yankelovich, after the Vietnam War the challenge to traditional values spread beyond the college campus to find a variety of expressions in larger society. This applied particularly to the ethic of self-fulfillment — the search for a full and rewarding life, replete with leisure, creativity and new experiences, vitality, and enjoyment. These were seen as a substitute for the orderly, work-centered ways of earlier decades. For many American adults, the central questions became: How can I find self-fulfillment? What kinds of commitments should I be making? What is worth sacrificing and how can I grow? Much more so than in earlier decades, intimate lifestyles became a matter of personal *choice,* and — at least before the emergence of AIDS in the 1980s — many choices seemed more available than they had been in the past, i.e., obtaining a divorce, experimenting with extramarital sex, staying single, trying out communal life, remaining childless, "swinging," cohabiting, celibacy, and casual sex — to name just a few.

Although many radical experiments that took place during the late sixties and early seventies attracted only small minorities of the population, the counterculture expanded the range of permissible norms by proposing such radical alternatives. Consequently, sanctions on relatively milder variations were reduced (Marciano, 1975). Indeed, important normative changes took place in the seventies in the United States. In general, the American public became more accepting and tolerant of many behaviors and lifestyles that were considered deviant or immoral in earlier times, such as a married woman being gainfully employed even if her husband was able to support her; deliberately remaining single; engaging in premarital sexual intercourse; husbands and wives taking separate vacations; living together as an unmarried couple; being married and deciding against children; and choosing to have children while being single. Also, for the first time in American history, only a minority of Americans expressed discomfort at having friends who were homosexuals, and in the single decade of the seventies the number of Americans who believed that both sexes should share responsibility for cleaning the home nearly doubled (from 24% to 42%). Furthermore, nearly two-thirds of Americans rejected the idea that parents should stay together for the children's sake, even if the partners were unhappy with each other. In general, it has become normal to think of marriage as not necessarily a permanent arrangement, and such notions make it much less stigmatizing for people to get a divorce. To summarize, in the seventies "Virtually all recent normative changes in America have moved toward greater tolerance, openness, choice and a wider range of acceptable behavior" (Yankelovich, 1982, pp. 85–86).

These normative changes have brought various lifestyle options within the reach of many more Americans than ever before. Even more so, because of some noticeable demographic shifts that have taken place since the sixties, most Americans are now directly affected by nontraditional lifestyles. When we conceive of traditional marriage and the family as *a lifelong relationship between a man and a woman, sanctioned by law, resulting in one or more children, with the husband as the sole breadwinner* (Macklin, 1987), then we must conclude that nontraditional family arrangements and options have penetrated deeply into mainstream American life. The following developments illustrate this conclusion: an increase in the age of first marriage (indicating a tendency to postpone marriage), leading to a situation in which a majority of adults between 20 and 24 are single; a divorce rate that doubled between 1965 and 1985, indicating that for about 40% of all Americans who get married nowadays, marriage is no longer a lifelong commitment, and that many children will live in single parent families or with step-parents during significant periods of their life; an increasing number of single households; a growing incidence of unmarried cohabitation among never-marrieds and divorced persons; an increasing participation of women in the labor force, making the single-earner family more an exception rather than a rule (less than one out of five employees is a man working to provide total support for his wife and children); the number of single-parent households has nearly doubled since 1970; an increasing rate of unwed parenthood; and an enhanced tendency to forsake parenthood (no less than ten million Americans decided to remain childless in the seventies). In addition, half of the marrieds (many more women than men) will become widow(er)s, and many will live out their lives in an alternative lifestyle, particularly singlehood. Throughout the life cycle, many American adults will experience several different lifestyles, including nontraditional ones such as the single parent family, the stepfamily, singlehood, and unmarried cohabitation (Sussman, 1975). Henry Etzkowitz and Peter Stein (1978) have suggested that there is no longer one steady, predictable life cycle pattern for the average adult in American society. Although some individuals adhere to the same lifestyle — whether traditional or variant — others move from more traditional patterns to more variant patterns and vice versa during their life cycle. According to Etzkowitz and Stein, more and more men and women are, at certain points in their lives, examining their options and making new decisions about the direction of their lives.

Despite all these changes in society, it must nevertheless be reiterated that there is not a single lifestyle that is, even by a sizable minority, viewed as preferable to marriage in the long run. Marriage continues to be the dominant *cultural ideal.* Thus, most cohabitors eventually marry, nearly all divorcé(e)s prefer to remarry after a few years (most actually do), singlehood is usually perceived as a temporary or involuntary lifestyle, while sexually open marriages and communes attract only tiny proportions of the population. For those few individuals who join communes, it tends to be a temporary stage, especially for youngsters in search of their identity. As many family sociologists have noted, marriage is too ubiquitous and deeply-rooted an institution to be rapidly transformed or replaced. Furthermore, changes in patterns of intimate human relationships are necessarily much slower than technological changes (Caplow et al., 1982). As Eleanor Macklin (1987, p. 317) emphasizes, the family is not disappearing, but "continuing its age-old process of gradual evolution, maintaining many of its traditional functions and structures while adapting to changing economic circumstances and social ideologies." This process merely accelerated during the late 1960s and early 1970s.

It is especially noteworthy that the quality of contemporary marriage and family life seems better than it ever used to be. While in the first half of this century husbands and wives led their own life in most marriages, and experienced difficulties in communicating with one another, the marital relationship nowadays is much closer and intimate. Spouses now tend to enjoy each other's company, their mutual interaction, and their sexual relationship. Morton Hunt (1974), for example, compared the data gathered by Alfred Kinsey and his associates (1948, 1953) during 1938–1949 with his own data, collected in 1972, and found that the quality of sexual relationship had improved considerably among American couples. Researchers Theodore Caplow and his associates (1982, p. 323), commenting on the changes in American marriage and family life since the 1920s, noted that

> ... we discovered increased family solidarity, a smaller generation gap, closer marital communication, more religion, and less mobility. With respect to the major features of family life, the trend of the past two generations has run in the opposite direction from the trend that nearly everyone perceives and talks about.

Furthermore, while societal changes concerning nontraditional lifestyles began in the sixties, and became integrated into society during the seventies, some changes, such as the divorce rate, have stabilized since the end of this last decade. In some respects, there even seems to be a refocus on more traditional values. The faltering economy in the beginning of the eighties, as well as the rapid proliferation of herpes, and especially AIDS, has had a dampening impact upon the willingness to experiment as well as upon the tolerance of various lifestyles and relationships. The easy way in which people in the sixties and seventies – often proudly – indulged in all kinds of experiments with group sex, swinging, bisexuality, and multiple sexual encounters seems far remote from today's reality in which many singles, marrieds, and gays have become rather reluctant to engage in casual sex out of fear of becoming infected with AIDS. This disease, "the most merciless health crisis in recent memory" (Queen, 1987), is having a tragic impact particularly upon the gay community where many people see their friends die and are living with the constant fear of having perhaps been infected years ago. Although the spread of AIDS among heterosexuals is not progressing as fast as was expected a few years ago, the fear of contracting this deadly disease has made many heterosexuals very wary of sexual contacts with unfamiliar people. In a recent study conducted at the University of Rhode Island, over 40% of the students reported that a concern over AIDS had affected their sexual behavior in some way. This was particularly true for the sexually active students (Carroll, 1988). In addition, several surveys have documented the increasing conservatism in sexual matters. For instance, in a study of New England students, it was found that from 1974 to 1979 virginity declined significantly for both men and women. Sex started earlier and was more likely to occur with a less committed partner, in line with more liberal sex philosophies. However, in 1986 there was more evidence of the restriction of sex to committed relationships, and the philosophy of sex had become significantly more conservative. For instance, in 1979 38.7% of the sample indicated that they had had their last sexual experience in a steady relationship; this figure rose to 73.8% in 1986. In general, the students of 1986 were more like those of 1974 in their sexual behaviors and attitudes than those in 1979. It was even noted that fewer men were sexually experienced in 1986 than in 1974 (Murstein et al., 1988).

VARIANT LIFESTYLES AND RELATIONSHIPS

Nontraditional family forms can occur within widely divergent social contexts. The sociologist Noel Cazenave (1980), in a discussion of lifestyles among low income blacks, made a distinction between "alternative" versus "alternate" lifestyles. In the first, there is an emphasis upon *ideologically-based* choices available to those who have the resources to move beyond traditional, normative patterns. This is, for example, the case with couples entering an open marriage arrangement, or individuals opting for "creative singlehood" (Libby, 1977). The word "alternate" is reserved by Cazenave for those arrangement that are not voluntarily chosen, but are often a consequence of *structural restraints*. For example, the prevalence of single parent families among black women living near the poverty level is, among others, associated with the lack of eligible black men, the welfare system, and the unavailability of Medicaid abortions. In a similar vein, Marciano (1975) noted that the word "deviant" is used to refer to such lifestyles where suffering and deprivation occurs, while the word "variant" is employed as a label for voluntary or intentional formations created with a relatively high degree of consciousness.

The issue of what type of factors induce individuals to enter a certain lifestyle is even more complex than the foregoing would suggest. First, even individuals in more fortunate circumstances than those who live below the poverty level often do not make a deliberate decision to become involved in a certain lifestyle. Many young couples seem to drift into cohabitation without much mutual discussion, and without any explicit decision. Second, sometimes a lifestyle is forced upon an individual by factors other than structural ones, as is the case with many gays and lesbians, with those who are widowed, or with those abandoned by a spouse. In these cases, the values, motives, and ideals of the individuals involved may be very much at odds with the actual lifestyle in which they find themselves. Third, individuals may decide to become involved in a certain lifestyle — such as a sexually nonexclusive marriage or living alone — not so much because they are pulled towards it, but because they feel pushed away from another lifestyle, such as a marriage that has gone sour.

In general, it is important to distinguish between (1) a particular *form* of a lifestyle that can easily be defined or observed, such as singlehood, nonmarital cohabitation, or communal households, (2) its *content*, i.e., the different behavioral patterns as well as the attitudes and values of the participants that may vary from normative disapproval to ideological commitment, and (3) the *context* of the lifestyle, i.e., the factors that lead a person to adopt that particular lifestyle, including factors within or outside the control of the person (Buunk, 1983). For example, the singlehood of someone who has just lost his or her spouse after thirty years of marriage is hardly comparable to that of the young professional who prefers singlehood to the obligations and restrictions of marriage. Also, the context of a secretive extramarital affair stemming out of dissatisfaction with marriage is different from that of the mate exchange engaged in by some "swinging" couples.

In this book we prefer the word *variant* lifestyles and relationships, to emphasize three points (cf. Sussman, 1975; Marciano, 1975). First, the word "variant" refers to the fact that this book focuses upon those lifestyles that are different from the sexually exclusive, legally sanctioned marriage couple that lives together in a joint household (cf. Swain, 1978; Macklin, 1987). Second, the word "variant" is used as a neutral term, instead of "deviant" or "alternative," acknowledging the many different meanings a certain lifestyle may have for the people involved, including those associated with Cazenave's (1980) terms "alternative" and "alternate." Because these last two meanings are not always easy to separate, and other meanings may exist, we employ the word *variant* to allow for all the possible contents and contexts of a given lifestyle. Finally, we included the word *relationship* in the title of this book to indicate a focus upon those lifestyles that imply ways for meeting needs of sexuality and intimacy that differ from those in a sexually exclusive marriage, and to make clear that there is a strong emphasis on these issues in our discussion of the various lifestyles.

The foregoing implies that this book does not deal with such lifestyles as stepfamilies, dual-earner and dual-career couples, and voluntary childless couples, although these are often seen as nontraditional family forms. To a certain extent, these lifestyles are indeed different from what was traditionally viewed as the ideal marriage and family, but as such they do not differ from other marriages in terms of meeting needs for intimacy and sexuality. We also do not discuss single parenthood, since a separate book in the Family Studies Text Series is devoted to this lifestyle. Thus, the lifestyles we deal with in this book include singlehood, nonmarital cohabitation, gay and lesbian lifestyles and relationships, sexually nonexclusive marriages, and communal arrangements, including the many different variations within these lifestyles.

For each of the lifestyles in this book, we shall discuss basically the same issues. The first issue we deal with is the question of how to *define* a particular lifestyle. This is an important issue, since self-definition is not adequate when we wish to define someone as being engaged in a given lifestyle. The lifestyle one is involved in is not necessarily a salient issue or an important part of one's self-concept. According to our definition, one can, for example, have a sexually nonexclusive marriage, or be single, but seldom think of oneself in this way. Little is known about the extent to which people include their lifestyle in their self-concept. The more one deviates from the social environment, or consciously chooses the lifestyle, the more we expect that the lifestyle is an important part of the self-concept. But in many cases it is the other aspects of one's life, such as personality traits, educational background, profession, and social class that are more salient in one's subjective identity.

After defining the lifestyle, we deal with the societal context, focusing primarily upon the prevalence of the lifestyle in society, as well as the attitudes towards it. When relevant, we discuss the societal discrimination of a lifestyle. Next we describe the varieties of the lifestyle that can be distinguished, particularly with respect to the way in which needs for intimacy and sexuality are met. Attention is then paid to the characteristics of the participants involved in the lifestyle — who they are in terms of their demographic and personality features. Throughout most chapters, we also discuss gender differences.

A special section in each chapter deals with the ways in which individuals become involved in that particular lifestyle, and why they remain in it. This issue includes not only the various pushes and pulls that make a given lifestyle a likely option but also those personal characteristics and structural factors that make a given lifestyle more or less difficult to attain. For example, structural factors such as a lack of available men may force many older women to remain single, while personality characteristics such as fear of commitment may keep individuals in the state of unmarried cohabitation. Each chapter also includes information about the negative aspects of each lifestyle, and about the well-being of the participants. Attention is paid to the specific problems encountered in that lifestyle, such as loneliness among singles, jealousy in sexually nonexclusive marriages, and lack of commitment in nonmarital cohabitation and communes. Finally, we shall compare American patterns with those in Western Europe, particularly in the Netherlands, when this offers further insight into the specific cultural context as represented by the United States. This also allows the reader to place the status of variant relationships in the United States into a broader perspective.

REVIEW QUESTIONS

1) What different conceptualizations of variant, nontraditional, or alternative lifestyles are apparent throughout the chapter?
2) What impact did the counterculture have upon American society?
3) Why are most Americans now affected by nontraditional forms of marriage and the family?

SUGGESTED PROJECTS

1) Interview your grandparents about what family life was like when they were young, and what the attitudes were towards different variant lifestyles. Compare this with the situation today, and make a list of similarities and differences.
2) Interview your parents or adults of that age about how they perceived the tumultuous late sixties and early seventies.
3) Discuss the impact that AIDS is having on the willingness to become involved in variant lifestyles.

CHAPTER
2
Singlehood

DEFINING SINGLEHOOD

THE TERM "SINGLE" evokes very divergent images. On the one hand, the concept has clear negative connotations, including those of the homely spinster, the pathetic divorcées and pitiful widows, and the lonely unattractive bachelors unable to find a mate. On the other hand, there are the stereotypes of the swinging, trend-setting singles, who actively pursue an exciting lifestyle packed with sexual variety, travelling, new experiences, freedom, and autonomy. In addition to evoking a variety of meanings, different criteria have been used to classify someone as single. While sometimes the term "single" is restricted to the never-married, this word is most often used to designate a global residual category comprising *all* adults who are not legally married: the divorced, the widowed, and the separated—whatever the nature of their living arrangements or intimate involvements may be (Stein, 1983). However, there are other definitions of singlehood that, in one way or another, refer to a person on his or her own. Thus, it is not uncommon to equate singlehood with living alone, or with being unattached, and it is often even implicitly assumed that all singles maintain a separate household.

While this last assumption is clearly unwarranted, it is beyond doubt that whether or not a person lives with an intimate partner is a rather crucial matter that has far reaching consequences—for the daily organization of a person's life, the availability of social support, and the opportunities for emotional and sexual intimacy. Therefore, in this chapter we shall deal particularly with those unmarried individuals who do not cohabit with an intimate partner, although they may share a residence with a friend, children, or relatives, and may have a more or less stable intimate relationship with someone living elsewhere. Unfortunately, the existing literature seldom pays attention to the living arrangements of unmarried people, which often makes it difficult to make statements about the group in which we are particularly interested. Nevertheless, in our discussion we shall exclude as much as possible those unmarried persons who live with an intimate partner in a joint household. Chapter 3 is devoted to cohabiting couples. Furthermore, we limit this chapter primarily to heterosexual singles, as lesbian and gay singles are discussed in Chapter 4. We also refrain from paying particular attention to older singles, but refer to Brubaker (1985) for more information about this group. Finally, the issue of single-parent families is, as stated before, not dealt with specifically in this book, although many of the issues discussed here apply to single parents as well.

SOCIETAL CONTEXT

Incidence in Society

Singles constitute a large part of the American adult population. The number of one-person households increased considerably in the seventies, and in 1985 approximately 30% of all American men and more than 35% of all American women over the age of eighteen were not residing with a partner. While many unmarrieds share their home with others — children, parents, or friends — nearly one out of four households in 1985 consisted of people living alone. Most of these men and women live in urban areas where multiple living complexes or neighborhoods can be found that are occupied primarily by people who are single. Particularly the group of younger never-marrieds has grown substantially over the past twenty years, a growth that in part reflects an increase in the young adult population as a consequence of the "baby-boom" in the years following World War II. The trend toward even more singles may, therefore, diminish within the next decades, as the divorce rate has levelled off. It should also be noted that, perhaps surprisingly, the percentage of the adult population that is unmarried is lower at the present time than it was at the beginning of this century. The percentage of unmarrieds in the total adult population gradually decreased from the turn of the century until the early sixties, but since then the trend has reversed.

An important factor behind the growth in the percentage of never-marrieds is the increased tendency to postpone marriage. Since the mid-fifties, men and women have increasingly entered into marriage at a later time in life. For example, the median age at first marriage for men increased from 22.5 years of age in 1956 (the lowest median marriage age recorded in the history of the United States) to 24.6 years of age in 1980; for women the shift was from 20.1 to 22.1 years. Among young adults, the increase in the percentage of unmarrieds has been dramatic. In 1985, the majority of individuals between the ages of 20 and 24 had never been married (men 75.6%; women 58.5%). Some 25 years earlier, in 1960, the situation was quite different: only 53.1% of the men and 28.4% of the women had not been married at that stage in their life. There are several reasons for the apparent increased incli- nation to postpone, or even to forsake, marriage, including the growth in the number of women enrolled in college, an increase in the number of career opportunities for women, a greater ambivalence regarding the desirability of marriage, the increasing availability and acceptability of birth control methods, as well as the increased popularity and accep- tance of unmarried cohabitation. In general, marriage has become less imperative and less of an automatic means through which to obtain children, mutual aid, and love (Libby, 1977). Although most of those who postpone marriage will indeed eventually get married, there is also an increasing — but still relatively small — number of people who will never marry at all, either because they can not find the right partner or because they deliberately opt for singlehood. It is nevertheless assumed that this will never be the case for more than 10% of the adult population (Cherlin, 1981). It must be emphasized that many of these will not be permanently single according to our definition, since they will cohabit during some period of their life.

In addition to the postponement and decreased popularity of mar- riage, the rising divorce rate has also contributed to the increased percentage of singles. The divorce rate more than doubled between 1960 and the beginning of the 1980s, and it is projected that 40% of all marriages of those born in the 1970s will eventually end in divorce (Glick and Norton, 1977). While in 1960 divorced individuals consti- tuted only 2.3% of the total adult population, this figure rose to 7.6% in 1985. Although most of the divorced — about five out of six men and three out of four women — eventually remarry, the remarriage rate underwent a slight decline in the seventies. This could, of course, merely mean a postponement of marriage. In any case, about half of all remarriages take place more than three years after divorce, which means that a similar proportion of divorcé(e)s will be unmarried for at least three years (Cherlin, 1981). This does not, of course, necessarily mean that they are living alone all this time, given the growing popularity of cohabitation among divorcé(e)s.

When we take into consideration all the developments described above, it seems likely that most Americans will spend a considerable part of their adult life as unmarried individuals, and that most will live alone during a period of their adult lives. This is especially true for women, who have, as will become clear later on, a much higher chance than men of becoming widowed. They also have a lower chance of finding a new partner while single. Nevertheless, the proportion of widowed in the total group of singles has decreased since 1960. The very few who will never live alone include those individuals who marry at the age of eighteen, and die before their partner does, or those who, from the moment they reach adulthood, move from one marital or cohabiting relationship into the other without interruption.

Although singlehood seems widespread in contemporary American society, by historical standards there is nothing unusual about the present situation, which is characterized by a high proportion of unmarried adults. For example, among the nobility and gentry in England at the end of the eighteenth century, more than 20% of the men and women who reached fifty had never been married. In 1773, *The Lady's Magazine* complained that "the men marry with reluctance, sometimes very late, and a great many are never married at all" (Stone, 1977, p. 242). Especially the younger sons remained bachelors, as they could not afford financially to get married. Although bachelors had the option of joining the army or service, "spinsters" had little choice other than to get married. As a consequence, attempts to marry off a daughter in the upper classes in the late nineteenth century, sometimes "turned into a desperate man-hunt" (Stone, 1977, p. 243).

Attitudes in Society

American attitudes toward singlehood have been quite negative in the past. In colonial America, due to the need to produce offspring, singlehood was a lifestyle penalized by higher taxes (Murstein, 1974). In the late fifties, a large majority of the American adult population (80%) still agreed that a woman must be either sick, neurotic, or immoral to remain unmarried. This attitude has changed drastically since then, and in 1978 only 25% held a similar viewpoint (Yankelovich, 1982). According to Leonard Cargan and Matthew Melko (1982), these changes are reflected in popular literature by the use of the neutral word "single," instead of the somewhat derogatory terms "bachelor" and "spinster," and in the increasing number of articles on singles. Furthermore, the topics discussed in these articles are now of a different nature. Although the problem of loneliness and the advantages of freedom can be found in writings on singles throughout the century, discussions of discrimination against singles, and a questioning of the normality of marriage, are now more commonplace than they were in the fifties. Additionally, a few decades ago many explanations for singlehood were mentioned that are barely considered as relevant today, such as religion, bad luck, illness, military service, prison, selfishness, lack of maturity, and dedication to parents. Thus, there was a focus on factors that supposedly interrupted the "natural" trajectory leading to marriage. Singlehood was not perceived to be a variant lifestyle, the result of a free choice that offered an individual certain desirable and "normal" goals. Another trend has been toward a more neutral, instead of value-laden, discussion of the intimate, work, and financial lives of single individuals, and of the ways they might find a spouse.

Nevertheless, descriptions of singles as basically deviant, immature, and sexually disturbed are still to be found. Social psychological studies have, indeed, shown that negative stereotypes of singles continue to exist. In one study, for instance, it was found that individuals living alone were evaluated less favorably, and were perceived to be less friendly, colder, less attractive, more private, less extroverted, and lonelier than those living with roommates. They were also evaluated as being less noisy, more independent, and busier (Parmelee and Werner, 1978). It is probable that the different categories of singles, such as the divorced and the never married, will be evaluated differently, depending also upon their age, gender, and sexual lifestyle. For example, a divorced, promiscuous woman in her thirties will evoke quite different images from a never-married, nearly celibate male bachelor of past forty. In any case, traditionally male and female singles have been viewed differently. As Leonard Cargan (1986) points out, with respect to the past in Western society, bachelors have been mostly stereotyped as leading carefree lives of unrestrained freedom, while single women were stereotyped as unattractive and unfortunate creatures deserving pity.

American attitudes towards singlehood may still be less positive than those found in other Western countries. While, as noted earlier, a fourth of the American population still considers an unmarried woman immoral or mentally disturbed, virtually all adults in the Netherlands approve of women living as singles. Furthermore, the impression that singles are not necessarily unhappier than married persons is gradually permeating public opinion. While in 1965, 60% subscribed to the view that one who is married is generally happier than one who remains single, this opinion was only expressed by 35% of the Dutch population in 1975, and by 1980 this percentage had dropped to 25% (Oudijk, 1983).

VARIETIES OF THE SINGLE LIFE

Aside from the formal distinction between the never-married, divorced, separated, and widowed, many different types of singlehood can be distinguished. As is the case in the following chapters, we shall focus here upon those typologies that are relevant from a social psychological point of view. The typologies to be discussed are based upon attitudes toward the state of singlehood and upon the various ways that needs for intimacy and sexuality are expressed. We shall first describe the classification that concerns the extent to which singlehood is viewed as a stable and voluntary lifestyle. Subsequently, we shall deal with a classification that revolves around the sexual lifestyles of singles.

Stability and Voluntariness

According to sociologist Peter Stein (1981, 1983), the heterogeneous group of singles can be categorized firstly by examining the voluntary versus involuntary character of their single state, and secondly by ascertaining to what degree their singlehood is seen as stable or temporary. On the basis of these dimensions, four types of singlehood can be distinguished. (Stein's typology is similar to the one developed by Arthur Shostak, 1987).

1) Voluntary and temporary singles. This category of singles comprises the never-marrieds and formerly marrieds who are open to the possibility of marriage or cohabitation, but who are not actively seeking a mate for a variety of reasons. These reasons include education, career, or the desire to experiment with relationships and lifestyles. Some individuals are simply postponing marriage, while others may elect to spend some time finding out whether they really do want to marry, and if so, what type of partner and marriage they prefer. For these individuals, dating enables experimentation and is a means of obtaining sexual gratification or companionship; its goal is not primarily to find a mate. Arthur Shostak (1987) describes such singles as "ambivalents."

2) Voluntary and stable singles. This group of singles, designated as the "resolved" by Shostak (1987), has chosen to be single, is generally satisfied with that choice, and tends to be committed to singlehood. It is not clear how many singles belong to this group, but in a recent Canadian study of 482 unmarried adults (Austrom and Hanel, 1985), it was found that nearly half considered themselves single by choice. These people were more positive toward single life than those who did not deliberately opt for the single status. Being single by choice does not necessarily mean that such a choice cannot change under certain circumstances. When, for example, a dedicated convinced bachelor unexpectedly falls head over heels in love, such an event can lead him to revise his earlier plan to remain single for the rest of his life. But the differences with the foregoing lifestyle lie in the more or less conscious decision to forsake marriage and lead a life as a single person. The factors contributing to such a decision can be quite diverse. There are those — in particular women — who opt for singlehood, not so much because they consider it to be an attractive lifestyle but more because marriage would interfere with their commitment to a career and upward mobility (Higginbotham, 1981). Others oppose the idea of marriage because it would represent a restriction of human growth, of freedom and autonomy, and of sexual availability (Adams, 1976). Finally, a rather different and particular group of voluntary stable singles includes priests and nuns.

3) Involuntary temporary singles. This category — referred to as "wishfuls" by Shostak (1987) — consists of those who would like to be married or live together and are actively seeking a future mate. These activities can include dating, frequenting singles' bars, signing up with dating services, or placing and answering personal ads (Simenauer and Carroll, 1983). This category includes not only many relatively young, never-married people, but also somewhat older men and women who were previously not interested in marriage, and only later decided to look for a mate, as well as many widowed and divorced individuals. As stated earlier, about half of the divorced remarry within three years (Cherlin, 1981). In general, among the widowed and divorced we encounter individuals who are dissatisfied with their single state and consider marriage to be the main road to personal fulfillment.

4) Involuntary stable singles. This group of singles is mainly made up of older divorced and widowed individuals who would prefer to remarry, but have, for various reasons, not been able to find a new mate. Many are unlikely to ever enter the state of matrimony again. In this category we also find older, never-married individuals who perceive their singlehood as undesirable, but who have more or less reluctantly come to accept singlehood as their most likely future lifestyle. The term "regretfuls" (Shostak, 1987) seems to characterize this group adequately. The group of involuntary stable singles includes people with a variety of characteristics. There are those whose physical or psychological state makes them rather unattractive as a potential mate, but this category also includes many well-educated, professionally very successful, and often attractive women. In an article with the provocative title "Where Are the Men for the Women at the Top?" Christine Doudna and Fern McBride (1981) called attention to the problems that women who have attained a high level of occupational success face in finding a mate. As shall be explained in detail later on, these problems are due mainly to the demographic fact of a lack of older single well-educated men.

It must be emphasized that the boundaries between the categories discussed above are fluid, and often difficult to determine. Some involuntary singles, for example, may go through alternating periods in which they view their singlehood either optimistically as temporary, or pessimistically as permanent. Furthermore, with regard to Stein's (1981, 1983) typology, it remains unclear how many years of involuntary singlehood need to have elapsed before the social scientist or the individual will consider it to be a stable state. In addition, the line between voluntary and involuntary is rather thin. For example, a substantial group probably remains single without ever making a conscious decision to do so, and may, after a number of years, come to the conclusion that they would find it rather difficult to adjust to married life. They subsequently decide to resign themselves to going through life as a single and are determined to "make the best of it."

Another qualification of this typology lies in the transitions between the various categories that people may make during their life cycle. For example, someone may, after a divorce, choose what is believed to be a state of voluntary stable singlehood, motivated by a reluctance to again become involved in a committed intimate relationship. After a number of years and having experienced the drawbacks of singlehood, however, there may be a change of mind, and efforts to find a new spouse are initiated — thus entering a state of involuntary temporary singlehood. When these efforts prove to be unsuccessful, he or she may end up in the category of the involuntary stable singles.

Sexual Lifestyles

Many different types of singlehood can be discerned, based upon how one's needs for intimacy and sexuality are met. They vary from the "swinging single" to the celibate priest. Two dimensions seem particularly important when describing the sexual lifestyles of singles. The first dimension is whether or not one has a steady, intimate relationship; the second is whether or not one has multiple sexual involvements. Four main types of singlehood can be distinguished on the basis of these dimensions.

1) Celibacy. Singles may be temporarily or permanently celibate and forsake all sexual contacts and relationships. According to Gabriele Brown (1980), there are several forms of celibacy. First, celibacy may be freely chosen by religious or spiritual men and women, stemming from a total commitment to a celibate life for the sake of a higher goal, often religious in nature. Celibacy may also be a transient state for the divorced and widowed, who feel they are not yet emotionally ready for a new relationship. Many singles may pass through a stage in which they lead a solitary existence except for friendships, refusing all dates and sexual contacts. Brown points out that some individuals become celibate in a more or less natural way, when their attention shifts from sex to other sources of enjoyment in life. Brown suggests that by being celibate one can concentrate more on deeper levels of love and tenderness, experiences that can easily become lost in sex. Nevertheless, much celibacy is of an involuntary nature, found among those unable, for whatever reason, to find appropriate sexual partners. It is not unlikely that some of these individuals will decide it is better not to expect sex at all, rather than to be frustrated most of the time. Those caught up in a deviant lifestyle that conflicts with their own norms and the standards extant in their social environment, may sometimes redefine their lifestyle in a positive sense and offer justifications instead of excuses. In addition, there are, of course, people who, because of past experiences or their upbringing, are not very interested in sex and in some cases even appalled by the thought of sexual contact.

Little is known about celibacy among singles. A study by Jacqueline Simenauer and David Carroll (1983) gives some idea of the prevalence of celibacy in this group. In their sample of over three thousand singles, ranging from twenty to fifty-five years of age, a total of 4% of the male and 9% of the female respondents indicated that they had had no sexual partners since becoming single. The largest category was widowed individuals, who were probably still traumatized by the death of their mates and did not feel emotionally prepared for a new relationship. Next came the never-married who were still without sexual experience, waiting for the right moment and person to come along. Other people without sexual experience included those without a sexual drive whatsoever (though this was rarely found), and older singles over forty years of age. Another interesting finding was that 5% of the men and 9% of the women who had been single all of their life had never had a sexual partner. Unfortunately, we do not know how many of these were younger people, and how many had been voluntarily and involuntarily celibate for a lengthy period of time. But other findings from this study suggest that this last category is hardly a negligible one: among those who had been single for a period of ten to thirty years, 4% of the men and 7% of the women had not had a sexual partner during that time. These data show that substantial periods of celibacy are far from rare among singles, especially among women. It seems likely that nowadays the fear of AIDS is fostering at least temporary periods of celibacy among many singles.

2) Casual sex. The sexual life of some singles consists mainly of "one-night stands" and short, uncommitted sexual relationships. According to Robert Staples (1981), in his study of black singles, the most common type of single is the free-floating single, who is unattached to another person and dates randomly with or without the aim of seeking a committed relationship. Peter Stein (1983) notes that sexual experimentation is a part of the identity of many singles, enjoyed for itself, or as a stage leading to marriage or to the choice of a single sexual partner. In addition, many divorced or separated individuals go through a period during which they engage in casual sex because it reassures them of their attractiveness, desirability, and sexual competence — areas in which their self-confidence is often shaken in a destructive relationship.

It is difficult to ascertain for how many singles casual sex is, or has ever been, the predominant sexual lifestyle. A Chicago sample found that total sexual freedom and licentiousness were not characteristic of most young singles (Starr and Carns, 1972). However, a study by Leonard Cargan (1986) showed that in America, New Zealand, and Australia, singles had had more sexual partners than their married counterparts. In the nationwide study by Simenauer and Carroll (1982), more than 20% of the men, but only around 5% of the women who had been single for at least three years, had been involved with fifty sexual partners or more. Many of these contacts must have been casual, since it is, of course, difficult to imagine how someone could have had that many, or even substantially fewer, meaningful long-term relationships. Indeed, many of the comments of these respondents reflected a history of casual sexual experiences. Singles do not, however, have a very positive view of casual sex as a stable sexual lifestyle: only 20% of the men and 6% of the women recommended this form of behavior. Those who praised it were predominantly found among the never-marrieds between twenty and thirty-four years of age, and, according to Simenauer and Carroll, "Much of the enthusiasm for casual sex and multiple involvements comes from young people who are just discovering the power of sex." Recently, the willingness to engage in casual sexual encounters has been dampened by the fear of acquiring AIDS. But aside from that, many singles oppose casual sex because it makes them feel empty afterwards; it is experienced as mechanical, without real emotions, and it makes some bored with sex. Interestingly, women described casual sex more as "lonely" or "dirty," while men were more inclined to characterize it as "meaningless" or "empty."

Nevertheless, the Simenauer and Carroll (1982) study showed that many sexual contacts among singles did take place between people who were not in love with each other. Although this pattern may have changed due to the fear of AIDS, it is still interesting to note that most singles in this study did not view love as a necessary condition for sex, and although many men claimed that they were in no real hurry, most slept with their dates in three evenings or less. Almost two-thirds of all men and one-half of the women indicated that they had sex on the first to third date. Many more women than men said that it usually took several months and meetings before they were ready for this step. Women often felt pressured to have sex early on and, when they did comply, it was often not for the sexual pleasure per se, but because they liked the man and were afraid of losing contact with him, or because they thought it was their own fault that they let it get to this point. Often, they felt more or less obligated to go further. The different perspectives of men and women, and a lack of communication, often cause problems in their interactions. For example, women accuse men of "always being on the make," while men misread friendly behavior as a sexual invitation.

3) Sexually exclusive relationships. These include the relationships between two single people with separate households, who have a more or less stable, committed relationship, but who for a number of reasons do not, or not yet, live together or marry. A different phenomenon is represented by arrangements where the partners explicitly refrain from living together, because of the value they attach to their autonomy or the fear of becoming involved in conflicts and day-to-day irritations once they enter into a living-together relationship (Straver, 1981). Little is known about the incidence, characteristics, and stability of such arrangements. Staples (1981), however, described what he called the "closed-couple relationship," an important pattern among black singles. In this case, the partners are oriented exclusively toward one another for their sexual and intimate needs, and fidelity is expected. There is no reason to assume why similar types of relationships are not prevalent among whites as well.

We must also mention in this context the more or less steady relationships some single women maintain with married men. According to Laurel Richardson (1986), who interviewed over 700 of what she refers to as "Other Women," such women have a different agenda from mistresses in the past. Today's single women want to finish their education, build a career, recover from a divorce, or explore their sexuality. Marriage or a comparable commitment may be seen as taking away valued time and energy that can be better spent on other, more desirable goals. On the other hand, such single women may still want a relationship with a man: "As an Other Woman, she believes she can have both." Contrary to the stereotype, sex is not the primary activity in these relationships. Instead, the focus is on intimacy — the talking, listening, and sharing. It needs to be noted that such relationships may not always be sexually exclusive for men, as many probably continue to have sex with their wives.

4) Sexually nonexclusive relationships. Relationships similar to the ones just described belong to this category, with the difference being that they are sexually open. A comparable variety of patterns, ground rules, and problems can probably be found here, as in the more or less stable arrangements in the sexually open marriages described in Chapter 5. Dutch sociologist Cees Straver (1981) describes an example of such a couple (not living together) that does not entertain a monogamous sex life, but disapproves of the development of a deep relationship with a third party. However, because the interdependency is much less here, and each partner has much more privacy, it may be easier to conduct such relationships without hurting the other person than in the case of marriage or cohabitation, and jealousy and relational conflicts can probably be avoided to a greater extent. Nevertheless, in the study of Simenauer and Carroll (1982), most singles indicated that they thought it was difficult or even impossible to be meaningfully and sexually involved with more than one person at the same time.

CHARACTERISTICS OF SINGLES

Single individuals are anything but a homogeneous group with respect to their demographic characteristics. There is a myriad of differences relating to age, sexual preferences, living arrangements, previous marital status, social class, ethnic background, and educational level. In fact, especially the younger singles offer — except, of course, for their marital status — a profile of American society as a whole. Here, we shall focus mainly upon the composition of the singles population in terms of age, marital status, and sex. Because of the way in which the available demographic data are published, we have to confine ourselves to all unmarried adults, including the ones possibly cohabiting.

The first noteworthy fact about the singles population is that a single person is more likely to be female: in 1985 there were eight million more single women than single men in this country. This large discrepancy is caused by the simple fact that there are more women than men in the United States for the reason that men, on the average, die 7.7

years earlier than women, and by the mathematical fact that the number
of married men and women is, of course, equal. As Figure 2.1 clearly
reveals, the larger number of female singles is not evenly distributed
over all categories. On the contrary, the male and female single populations differ substantially in their composition. First, despite the
greater number of female singles, many more men than women belong
to the never-married. More than 66% of the male singles have never
been married, compared to only about 40% of the female singles. This
discrepancy is due to the fact that, on the average, men marry two years
later than women. One must realize, however, that with increasing age
the percentages of never-married men and women approach one another. Among those who are sixty-five years of age and older, an even
higher percentage of women than men belong to the never-married.
Second, there are many more divorced and separated individuals in the
single-women category than there are among single men. This is largely
due to the higher remarriage rate of divorced men with younger, unmarried women. Last, but not least, Figure 2.1 shows the dramatic sex
difference in the prevalence of single widowhood — there are over five
times as many unmarried widows as unmarried widowers.

Among blacks, we encounter a somewhat different situation. First,
many more blacks remain unmarried for a substantial period of their
life. Even among the adults in the thirty-five to forty-four year range,
proportionately more than twice as many blacks as whites have not been
married. Interestingly, however, many blacks do get married later in
life. We see that for blacks over sixty-five, the proportion never-married
is only slightly lower than that for whites, while black women even
surpass their white counterparts in this area. Nevertheless, if present
trends continue, the majority of black adults will be unmarried in the
year 2000 (Stein, 1981; Staples, 1981).

While the younger singles are quite representative of the American
population as a whole, certain shifts can be identified in the categories
of men and women who remain unmarried as time passes. Among the
never-married men over the age of thirty, particularly the lower educated, blue collar workers are overrepresented, while among women
exactly the opposite is true: the better educated women with successful
careers tend to be single. In an extensive study, Spreitzer and Riley
(1974) found that 25% of the women, as opposed to 11% of the men,
with some college education had never been married. Another finding
was that the most intelligent men were *least* likely to remain unmarried,
whereas the most intelligent women were *most* likely to remain single.
Similar patterns were found in the area of occupational attainment. As
the well-known sociologist Jessie Bernard (1973) puts it: the never-

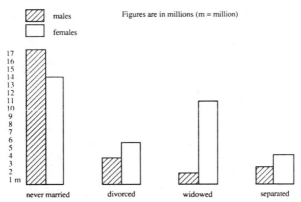

Figure 2.1 Marital status of the total unmarried U.S. population. Age 18 and over, 1980

Source: Stein (1983).

married men represent the "bottom of the barrel" and the never-married women the "cream of the crop." Two explanations have been offered for this phenomenon. First, it has been suggested that males, with their active role in the courtship process, evade women with strong, independent personalities. Second, it has been proposed that the better educated, occupationally successful women are less willing to enter marriage, perhaps out of fear of being trapped in the traditional role of wife and mother. Indeed, singlehood seems to promote occupational achievement among women, particularly because they do not have to deal with the role conflicts that can arise between work and family. A study by Sharon Houseknecht, Suzanne Vaughan, and Anne Statham (1987) shows that women who remained single throughout graduate school achieved more professional success than those women who had married prior to the completion of graduate school.

The characteristics of the different categories of singles described earlier in terms of voluntariness and stability of the lifestyle remain somewhat obscure. It is often supposed that singlehood is likely to be a voluntary choice, particularly among better educated, upper middle class people (Libby, 1977), and the foregoing would suggest that this may be especially true for women. Stein (1981) reviews some evidence that those who voluntarily choose singlehood, whether they have been married or not, are more liberal, permissive, and accepting of change. A Dutch study, however, found that creative singles (those who did not miss an intimate partner in their life) were not distinct in terms of educational and professional status. It was also found they were socially less active, but more involved than other singles with their neighbors.

More significantly, a creative single was more likely to be female. The few creative singles among the male population were much younger than those among the women (DeJong-Gierveld, 1980).

Little is known about the attitudes of singles, when compared to marrieds. There is some evidence that never-marrieds have more permissive attitudes toward many controversial social matters, such as the legalization of marijuana, homosexuality, pre-marital sex, and women's liberation. In addition, at least a minority of singles subscribe to negative views of marriage, seeing it as an enemy of individualism or an unromantic choice made largely under economic duress (Shostak, 1987). Of course, such opinions are not very likely among those singles who are eager to get married.

BECOMING AND STAYING SINGLE

If one were to ask a person why he or she was, or remained, single the answer would often not be worded in terms that emphasize all the benefits and potential for personal fulfillment of the single life, and the particular suitability of singlehood to one's needs and values. In many cases, becoming single is not an explicit, deliberate choice. This is, of course, self-evident for the widowed. Research on widowhood has shown that immediately after the death of a spouse, the survivor finds him or herself in a crisis and tends to become isolated, although children, relatives, and friends often offer considerable social support. After about six months, the widowed individual usually starts organizing his or her own life as a single person, developing a new identity and coping with the specific issues of life as a single person (Brubaker, 1985). Older widows often have little choice but to stay single, given the shortage of available men.

But it is not only for the widowed that single life represents a less than deliberate choice for a valued lifestyle. It is also true for many divorcé(e)s and separated individuals who are often alienated from an unsatisfactory relationship rather than attracted by the single life. Many of these singles would rather be married than single, and do not feel they are involved in the kind of lifestyle that suits them best. In addition, young people who are temporarily single do not often choose this lifestyle. Being immersed in a situation where most other young people are also single, there are simply few reasons to reflect upon one's single status and to come up with reasons for remaining single. Even among many people who have been unmarried all of their lives, other factors than one's motives and needs have been the predominant factors in remaining single.

As is the case with other lifestyles, singlehood should not be seen primarily as a stable choice stemming from deep motives within the person, but as an equilibrium between several forces acting upon that person. These factors include intrinsic pulls and pushes, structural and personal barriers, and alternative pulls and pushes. These last factors particularly concern the positive and negative aspects perceived to be inherent in marriage or cohabitation. Pushes in this direction may include emotional attachment and security, desire for children, social approval and prestige, career opportunities, and regular sexual satisfaction. Pulls away from marriage, which may drive people into singlehood, or make them want to stay single, include marital conflicts and tensions, fear of an unhappy marriage, obstacles to self-development, restricted availability of new experiences, boredom, and the fear of becoming involved in traditional sex roles (e.g., Adams, 1976; Libby, 1977; Stein, 1973).

Structural factors may play an important role in remaining single, especially for women over thirty. In the earlier mentioned article by Christine Doudna and Fern McBride (1979), the authors note that there are 128 single women for every 100 single men in the age group of thirty to thirty-five year olds, a gap that continues to widen with increasing age. But even these ratios underestimate the problematic situation for single women who are eager to marry. There is a traditional tendency for women to want men who are older, more successful and better educated than they are, while men want just the reverse. Women in their thirties, for instance, also have to compete with women in their late twenties, or focus on the few unmarried men in their forties. What has been called the "marriage squeeze" makes the situation even worse: for women who were born after World War II, at a time when the birth rate accelerated, there are not enough slightly older men available (Norton and Glick, 1979). The situation is particularly troublesome for better educated and occupationally successful women, since, as pointed out above, the men who are the most available are the least educated. Thus, many very successful women are single because of structural factors, and may not be able to realize the desired state of matrimony.

Structural constraints favoring singlehood especially exist for black women. According to Noel Cazenave (1980) and Robert Staples (1981), the pool of eligible black men is even lower, due to such factors as the relatively high mortality and crime rates among black men, the disproportionate number of black men in prisons, the higher rates of homosexuality and interracial marriage among black men as compared to black women, and the fact that black women are, on the average, better educated than black men (although there are many more black women than men in the lower classes as well). Another factor favoring single-hood among black women is the commitment to upward mobility, which is viewed as incompatible with marriage (Higginbotham, 1981). Indeed, a study of black college students showed that more women preferred to remain single rather than enter into a long-term marriage, while the reverse was true for men (Rao and Rao, 1980).

A second type of barrier that may keep people single is those personal capacities and characteristics that make certain individuals less attractive to others, or less capable of making contacts and building relationships. These features include unattractive characteristics, bad habits, emotional problems (including depression and neurosis), low self-esteem, negativistic attitudes (such as hostility and pessimism), fear of commitment and intimacy, inadequate social skills (including shyness), low assertiveness, and insufficient communication abilities. In this context, Robert Hansson, Warren Jones, and Bruce Carpenter (1984) have proposed the concept of "relational competence" to refer to the totality of an individual's characteristics that facilitate the acquisition, development, and maintenance of mutually satisfying relationships. Lack of such competence may make it difficult for singles to meet and build relationships with potential spouses.

Many of those who never marry seem to go through a period of great difficulty in their late twenties, when the number of singles decreases dramatically (Adams, 1976). At a time when more and more of one's friends get married, and the single person gradually becomes an exception in his or her social environment, the pulls of marriage can become very strong. Some will put a lot of effort into trying to find a mate, while others may feel themselves more or less forced to come up with arguments or motives explaining their lifestyle. Some may offer excuses (e.g., "I just haven't had the time to look for a mate yet," "It doesn't fit in with my career plans right now"), while others will seriously question which lifestyle they prefer, subsequently opt for singlehood, and develop a set of justifications supporting singlehood, stressing the positive aspects of this lifestyle.

The mid-thirties are a very critical period, particularly for childless single women, given the pending biological deadline for bearing children. Becoming a mother may become a matter of now-or-never. Although a small minority may opt for unwed motherhood, most prefer to get married. Given the lack of available men, this may be a very trying and desperate period for many single women. For single men in their thirties, the situation is different. In a study of late-marrying bachelors,

Jon Darling (1981) found that these men tended to be insulated from the normal peer group pressure to date during their adolescent years. Later on, they were committed to their parents, friends, or career. The death of a parent was often a kind of turning point in their life that made them consider marriage seriously for the first time. We again see that factors other than the intrinsic attraction of the lifestyle play an important role in remaining single.

According to voluntary permanent singles, the pulls of singlehood include better career opportunities (especially for women, see Houseknecht et al., 1987), availability of sexual experiences, exciting lifestyle, variety of experiences, freedom to change, economic, psychological and social autonomy, and the potential for developing friendships (Simenauer and Carroll, 1982; Libby, 1977). Of the various advantages, the ones mentioned most often — by about half of all singles — are mobility and freedom (Simenauer and Carroll, 1982). Such factors can thus be seen as the attractive side of singlehood, and these are also often recognized by married people. Indeed, throughout this century, freedom has recurrently been mentioned as a major advantage in popular articles on singlehood (Cargan and Melko, 1982).

HEALTH, WELL-BEING, AND LONELINESS

In the foregoing, some of the advantages of singlehood have been pointed out as they are perceived by singles and marrieds. As illustrated in Figure 2.2, however, singlehood is by no means without its problems. These problems include: loneliness; a restricted sexual and social life, plus the efforts one has to go through to have company during weekends; the stress of juggling ever-shifting commitments; the uncertainty of the commitment of others; the lack of role clarity; the tendency to become rigid; the dating grind; nobody to lean on; lack of social support and security, social and cultural discrimination, the social stigma of not being married; and feeling excluded from the world of married couples (Stein, 1981; Cargan and Melko, 1982; Simenauer and Carroll, 1982).

Loneliness

According to Stein (1983), the major tasks facing single adults are those faced by most adults, including seeking and finding productive work, maintaining emotional and physical well-being, adjusting to aging, building friendships, achieving intimacy, and fulfilling sexuality. However, in contrast to other issues, loneliness particularly is a prob-

ADVANTAGES

Woman: "You can do what you want, when and how you want. You don't have to stick to a meal schedule, share a bathroom, etc. If you want to be sloppy it's okay. If you're too lazy to wash the dishes, hang up clothes, no one will know. You plan your social life the way you like it. You have responsibility only for yourself. Whee!!"

Man: "Since becoming single and being alone a lot I have taken up pottery, read much more, thought thoughts I'd never considered before. None of this was possible when I was living with the same woman for such a long time. Living with someone takes away a lot of your creative energy."

Woman: "I feel living alone is better because I'm not always having to give in to male chauvinist ideas. I feel many times I'm being tested. Not by men but by Jesus! That's a wonderful thing to know, and it couldn't happen if I lived with someone else."

Man: "I can have anyone over to my apartment that I choose since I live alone. No one to answer to. The right to be private with the person when I wish."

DISADVANTAGES

Woman: "The major problem for me is the absence of someone to come home to. To hold in bed at night and make calming love to. Sex is a major part of my life, and I'm finding it hard to find good sexual experience and sometimes sex at all."

Man: "I do not believe in one-night stands in slam-bam-thank-you-Mam kind of love-making. I am a very choosy person. Therefore I am almost a celibate person most of the time, and this is one of the hardest things."

Woman: "Companionship, someone to know on a continuing basis, to have sex with, to help with repairs, someone to hug me now and then — I'm terribly lonely."

Man: Since I lived with a girl for so many years the hardest part of being alone is coming home each night and finding no one waiting for me. The house is empty. Everything is exactly in the same place where I left it in the morning. That's spooky — nothing has changed — there's no life."

Figure 2.2 Advantages and disadvantages of singlehood

Source: Simenauer and Carroll (1982).

lem confronting singles. Despite the change in attitudes toward single-hood, loneliness has continually been described in popular articles throughout this century as an important issue with which singles have to deal (Cargan and Melko, 1982). In the Simenauer and Carroll study (1982), loneliness was mentioned more often than any other problem; 42% of the single men and 44% of the single women perceived it to be the greatest disadvantage of being single. Although being alone can be experienced positively, loneliness is an aversive emotional experience. In a study by Philip Shaver and Carin Rubinstein (1980), four clusters of feelings characterized loneliness: 1) *desperation* (feeling desperate, panicky, helpless and abandoned); 2) *depression* (feeling sad, depressed, empty, sorry for oneself, and alienated); 3) *impatient boredom* (feeling uneasy, impatient, and bored; unable to concentrate); and 4) *self-depreciation* (feeling unattractive, stupid, and insecure). Loneliness must be distinguished from objective social isolation or the absence of social relationships. Some people may not have much need for social contact, and, although they have few friends, seldom feel lonely; others may be married, involved in a large social network, and still feel lonely because they do not feel accepted and understood by others. As these examples illustrate, loneliness is supposed to result from discrepancies between the actual and desired quantity and quality of social relationships. Loneliness is thus most likely to occur when someone has fewer relationships than he or she desires, or has relationships that lack certain desired qualities, such as intimacy, caring and understanding (Peplau and Perlman, 1982). According to Robert Weiss (1973), two basic forms of loneliness exist: *emotional* isolation, which results from the absence of an intimate partner, and *social* isolation, which is the consequence of the absence of supportive friends and ties to a social network. Weiss suggests that emotional isolation is not entirely alleviated by friends, kin, or coworkers, and that even a satisfying intimate relationship does not resolve social isolation. From this perspective, singles without an intimate partner may still feel lonely, even when they have a large and varied social network. There is some evidence, however, that social isolation is not more of a problem for singles than it is for marrieds. In a study by Duane Alwin, Philip Converse, and Steven Martin (1985), it was even found that people living alone were no less attached outside the household, and frequently exhibited higher levels of social connectedness than persons living with others.

While singles may cope with emotional isolation temporarily by reading, working, listening to music, spending money, or calling a friend (Shaver and Rubinstein, 1980), many singles look for a more permanent solution and engage in the active seeking of an intimate partner. Barkas (1980) has described many mechanisms singles may use to find dates. The most frequent mechanisms were informal situations, including parties, friends, school, hobbies, or interests. Less frequent were clubs, bars, and answering or placing an advertisement. Least used were the professional introduction services and special singles clubs and resorts.

Health and Well-being

The various categories of singles and marrieds have not only been compared with regard to loneliness, but also with numerous other indicators, including well-being and depression, admission to mental hospitals, suicide risk, illnesses (such as TB, cirrhosis of the liver, cancer, and coronary disease), and morbidity and mortality rates. Although the findings have not always been consistent, and many studies suffer from methodological shortcomings, the convergence of findings stemming from a large body of research allows for the following conclusions (for reviews see Anderson and Braito, 1981; Argyle and Henderson, 1985; Bloom, Asher, and White,1979; Stroebe and Stroebe, 1986).

1) The unmarried tend to be considerably less healthy physically and mentally than the married. Compared with the marrieds, more singles in the Cargan and Melko (1982) study mentioned nightmares, irrational fears, crying spells, worries and anxiety, guilt feelings, despondency, sexual apathy, loneliness, and feelings of worthlessness. Reviewing many studies, Walter Gove (1972a, 1974) concluded that never-marrieds have higher rates of mental illness than marrieds, and that singles generally have mortality rates that are one-and-one-half to two-and-one-half times higher than among marrieds.

One explanation for such differences concerns only the divorced and the never-married. According to this reasoning, it is not singlehood that causes low well-being, but rather the reverse. It is assumed that less well-adjusted persons have more difficulty in finding a mate and keeping a marriage intact — an explanation that is in line with what we noted in the last section with respect to the role of relational competence as a barrier for keeping persons in the state of singlehood. Support for this hypothesis is offered in a study by Spreitzer and Riley (1974), who showed that remaining unmarried was clearly associated with poor family life situations during childhood. The never-married scored relatively high on an index of childhood family pathology, comprising such variables as the quality of the relationships in, and the stability of, the family.

Although there is at least some truth to this line of thought, the most important factor explaining the lower well-being and health of singles seems to be the fact that singles lack social support from a partner (i.e., the spouse in most studies) who would promote health and well-being in several ways. First, such support may provide a protective shield, acting as a buffer and facilitating one's capability to cope with stressful life events. Second, partnership interaction may have a direct positive effect upon well-being by offering companionship, empathy, caring, love, and feedback. Indeed, singles and marrieds alike see the advantages of marriage in these terms. Finally, marriage may offer social regulation and structure in one's daily affairs, and the promotion of health-sustaining behaviors (Rook, 1984).

2) In most cases, the mental and physical health of the divorced and separated has been found to be the worst among those who are unmarried, followed by the widowed, and then by the never-married. Walter Gove (1974) described how for most causes of death, such as homicide, pedestrian accidents, cirrhosis of the liver, lung cancer, and leukemia, the divorced had higher mortality rates than the widowed, followed by the never-married. However, this pattern was not established for some other causes of death. For instance, widows were somewhat less likely than never-married women to die of diabetes and slightly more likely than divorced women to die in a motor accident. Nevertheless, in general, the differences between the various categories of singles follow the pattern described above.

It is not difficult to understand why the well-being of the divorced and widowed is worse than that of the never-married. In both cases, people have to go through a grief process and are confronted with the transition from being married to being single. Living alone, after having lived with a partner for a lengthy period of time, requires considerable adjustment. It is often difficult to maintain earlier, couple-based friendships, and, consequently, new relationships have to be initiated and built. Moreover, adapting to a different, lower social status can be a painful process.

But why are the divorced worse off than the widowed? There may be several reasons for this. There is more of a stigma attached to being divorced. Also, the divorced probably receive less support and understanding from others; friends of the divorced may side with the former spouse. At least as important is the fact that many divorcé(e)s have to deal with feelings of failure and rejection. Furthermore, as suggested before, it may also be true that obtaining a divorce is partially a consequence, instead of a cause, of mental problems (Stroebe and Stroebe, 1986). In this context, it is noteworthy that in Cargan and Melko's (1982) study, the divorced were less inclined to report loving and warm relationships with their parents during their youth. They more often tended to report conflicting and cold relationships and were also more likely to remember that neither parent was open toward them. In addition, they felt closed off from communication with their mothers.

Despite a general low level of well-being, adjustment to divorce is easier for certain categories of divorcé(e)s than for others. For example, the individuals who took the initiative to divorce, who are embedded in social networks, and who have a satisfying, intimate relationship, are relatively better off. In addition, certain personality characteristics, including high self-esteem, independence, tolerance for change, and egalitarian sex-role attitudes facilitate coping with the situation of being divorced (Price-Bonham, Wright, and Pittman, 1983).

3) In general, unmarried men are in poorer mental and physical health than unmarried women. There are numerous studies employing divergent criteria that have established gender differences in well-being and health among singles. It is striking that gender differences among the married often go in the opposite direction. For instance, Dutch sociologist, Jenny de Jong-Gierveld (1980) found that unmarried men were lonelier than unmarried women, but that married women were lonelier than married men. Gove (1972b) found a similar pattern with regard to suicide rates: the order from highest to lowest was single men, single women, married women, and married men.

Several factors seem to contribute to such gender differences among the unmarried: the larger availability of intimate friendships for unmarried women (especially women-women relationships), the fact that women may be equipped with more instrumental skills (e.g., cooking, housekeeping) that are important in terms of managing a single household, and, last but not least, the fact that the more socially advanced women, but the less well-adjusted men, tend to remain single. With regard to this last factor, it is noteworthy that one study showed that never-married men had relatively poor childhood relations with *all* other family members (father, mother, siblings), while among never-married women this was only true for the relationship with the mother. Furthermore, the parents of never-married men had been divorced much more often than those of never-married women (Spreitzer and Riley, 1974). The more problematic family backgrounds of never-married men may be partially responsible for their lower degree of mental health. However, the fact that widowed and divorced men also suffer more than their female counterparts points to the fact that factors other than those mentioned above, particularly the ability to cope in various ways with life as a single person, must also play a role.

The Importance of an Intimate Partner

Notwithstanding the foregoing, the categorization of individuals into two groups: singles and marrieds, is an oversimplification that ignores the multiple differences that can exist in the area of social relationships within each group. This is especially the case with respect to the question of whether one lives with a partner or not, and the issue of the quality of the relationship. A study by Jenny DeJong-Gierveld (1986) illustrates the importance of these factors. She found that in 1985, no less than 42% of unmarried adults in the Netherlands were involved in a steady partner relationship, mostly involving cohabitation. Although the unmarried tended to have higher loneliness scores than the married, this difference was completely due to the unmarrieds without an intimate partner; unmarried individuals involved in a partner relationship expressed low levels of loneliness similar to those of married individuals. This research confirms the notion that it is indeed the "true singles," as defined in this chapter, who are far more lonely than "single" people living together with an intimate partner. In terms of the relative absence of loneliness, it does not make a difference whether one is married or cohabiting. However, the presence of a spouse or cohabiting partner, as such, was not (in this study) a sufficient condition to prevent loneliness. Lower levels of loneliness were recorded for those who indicated that their partner was the first confidant, and who described their relationship as intimate, than for those who indicated this was not the case. Thus, as Weiss (1973) suggests, in order to be free of emotional loneliness, one seems to need at least one close, intimate relationship. Unfortunately, most studies that focus on the well-being of singles, as compared to married people, do not take into account the nuances made by De Jong-Gierveld.

REVIEW QUESTIONS

1) Why has the number of singles increased over the past decades?
2) List three different ways of classifying singles.
3) Describe the factors that may lead to singlehood and keep people in the state of singlehood.
4) Summarize what is known about the mental health of the various categories of singles. Discuss the explanations for these differences.

SUGGESTED PROJECTS

1) Interview a single man and a single woman over thirty-five. What do they consider to be the positive and negative aspects of their lifestyle? Do they wish to get married? Do they perceive problems in finding a suitable partner?
2) Visit a typical single's bar. Interview a man and a woman about their attitudes towards casual sex. Do they enjoy it? How do they feel afterwards? How do they deal with the risk of AIDS and other sexually-transmitted diseases?
3) Interview a married man and a married woman. What do they think are the advantages and disadvantages of being married versus being single?

Nonmarital Cohabitation

DEFINING NONMARITAL COHABITATION

A WIDE RANGE OF TERMS has been used to designate the phenomenon of nonmarital cohabitation, such as shacking-up, trial marriage, living together, living in sin, concubinate, consensus marriage, unmarried couples, living as husband and wife, and semimarriage. Partly because of this, considerable confusion exists as to what exactly constitutes cohabitation. Researchers have employed rather divergent criteria to define couples as cohabiting, including living under marriagelike conditions, maintaining a common residence, sharing finances and household duties, being together for a given number of months, having a sexual relationship, sleeping together for at least a certain number of nights a week, or simply perceiving oneself as being in a living-together arrangement (Cole, 1977; Newcomb, 1981).

Cohabitation cannot simply be defined as "marriage without being married." In many instances, the definition of a cohabital relationship is explicitly different from that of marriage. Thus, for some cohabiting couples, their lifestyle is *not yet* a marriage: it constitutes a sort of engagement period and preparation for marriage. Quite in contrast, other couples view their lifestyle as *not* a marriage *at all:* they oppose marriage and view cohabitation as an alternative to the state of matrimony. We favor a neutral definition that allows for such diverse meanings, and use the term *nonmarital cohabitation* to refer to all those unmarried, heterosexual couples with an intimate, sexual relationship, who share a common residence.

A specific form of cohabitation, which shall not be discussed here, is common-law marriage. This type of cohabitation dates back to the pioneering days when men and women sometimes did not have the opportunity to get married because of the absence of a priest or authorized official. In order to grant the couple all of the official rights and duties attached to marriage, the law allowed the couple to enter the marital state while awaiting a later-to-be-performed official ceremony. Some fifteen U.S. states still legally recognize such an arrangement. In contrast to common-law marriage, however, cohabiting participants do not view themselves as being married. Furthermore, cohabitation is a voluntary choice in a situation where there *is* an opportunity to get legally married if one should decide to do so.

SOCIETAL CONTEXT

Incidence in Society

Nonmarital cohabitation is hardly a typically modern phenomenon, nor an occurrence characteristic of Western culture. In many societies, both present and past, a distinction has been made between marriage as an institution integrated into, and controlled by, society and the less honored, less regulated, and less respected cohabitational union. In a well-known, vivid account of life in a medieval village, the French historian Emmanuel Le Roy Ladurie (1980) estimates that at least 10% of the couples were "living in sin." Cohabitation was commonplace in those days and was largely tolerated because of the value of dowries, the restrictions against marriage across class and faith lines, and the overriding need not to risk family property by rash and costly alliances. Marriage was not held in high esteem in the Middle Ages and was mainly seen as a business arrangement. Partially under the influence of the Reformation, marriage gradually came to be more positively valued, while living together without being married increasingly came to be viewed as a deviant lifestyle practiced either by the most impoverished, or, in some cases, the avant-garde (Macklin, 1983).

In general, until the end of the sixties, cohabitation in Western society was predominantly associated with the lower classes. Since then, however, cohabitation on the college campus and among the better educated has become more widespread. Parallel to this changing character of cohabitation, society has witnessed a veritable explosion in the number of individuals cohabiting between 1970 and 1980. For instance, from 1970–1980, the percentage of couples who had cohabited before marriage, in one selected county in Oregon, rose from 13% to 53% (Gwartney-Gibbs, 1986). Graham Spanier (1983) has linked the contemporary increase in cohabitation rates to greater tolerance of nonconventional behavior, the propensity of modern youth to delay marriage, the reduction in fertility, and a delay of first childbearing. Because of such developments, authors like Koray Tanfer (1987) and James White (1987) claim that this lifestyle is gradually becoming an institutionalized part of the mate selection process in America. While the total number of cohabiting couples in the United States tripled during the 1970s, according to census data, the rate of increase has slackened somewhat since 1980, although there is still a continual growth (Figure 3.1). Karay Tanfer (1987) comments that these census figures might distort the actual incidence of cohabitation. It is quite possible that the increase between 1970 and 1980 is due to more honest reporting because of a more tolerant climate of opinion. Moreover, the baby-boom cohorts are now in the age category when cohabitation is most likely.

The approximately two million couples — four million individuals — that the census reported to be cohabiting in 1985 represent 4% of all married and unmarried couples living together at that time in the United States. However, since most cohabitors eventually marry or breakup, currently cohabiting rates are always lower than "ever cohabiting rates." Therefore, many more than four million Americans must have cohabited at some point in their lives. Illustrative in this context is the study by Jacqline Simenauer and David Carroll (1982), conducted among more than three thousand unmarrieds, which showed that nearly half of this group had lived together with someone of the opposite sex.

The rise in cohabitation rates is not equally attributable to all age and marital status categories. Census figures show that the number of people cohabiting above the age of 65 has declined significantly since the early 1970s (Figure 3.1). This is probably caused mainly by changing social security laws that have made cohabiting less advantageous for senior citizens. In any case, while the majority of cohabiting couples was older than 45 in 1970, nearly two-thirds of the cohabitors were between 25 and 45 years of age in 1985. It is especially for this age group that cohabitation has rapidly become more popular over the past decade. Furthermore, while prior to the mid-seventies few cohabiting households included children (Spanier, 1983), between 1975 and 1986 the number of cohabiting couples with children in their household increased significantly (to some 30% of all cohabiting couples in 1986). Most often these unions included children from a previous marriage; nowadays, in about half of all cohabital arrangements, one or both partners are separated or divorced.

In line with the relaxation of college housing policies and dorm regulations, a rapid proliferation of cohabitation has taken place among college students. Depending on the colleges and universities surveyed, and the criteria used for what constitutes cohabitation, it is estimated that anywhere between 15% and 35% of all students have cohabited at some time or other during their lifetime (Cole, 1977; Macklin, 1983). Despite this increased visibility of cohabitation among students, its highest incidence can still be found among lower-class whites and

	1970	1980	1985
Number of couples	523	1,589	1,983
Under 25 yrs old	55	411	425
25-44 yrs old	103	837	1,203
45-64 yrs old	186	221	239
64 yrs or older	178	119	116
No children under 15 yrs	327	1,159	1,380
1 or more children under 15 yrs	195	431	603

Figure 3.1   Number of unmarried heterosexual couples in the United States (in thousands) and some selected characteristics

Source: U.S. Bureau of the Census.

blacks. A study by Richard Clayton and Harwin Voss (1977) revealed that nearly twice as many blacks as whites (29% versus 16%) reported they had cohabited in the past, and that individuals with less than a high school education indicated more often than those with a college education that they had lived together (23% versus 17%). A more recent study by Tanfer (1987), using a national survey of unmarried women, confirms an educational gap, but also shows that white women now score almost identical to black women with respect to cohabitation rates.

Cohabitation is more prevalent in certain regions. The highest percentages of cohabiting couples have been found in urban areas in the Northeastern United States and especially in the West. This is not a surprising finding since the West Coast and other heavily urbanized areas have a more tolerant social climate with respect to unconventional behavioral patterns. These regions offer more opportunities to engage in variant lifestyles without, for instance, being subjected to numerous familial and neighborhood pressures to lead a traditional life.

Although it is possible that nonmarital cohabitation will become much more prevalent in the United States in the future than it is today, it remains doubtful whether cohabitation rates in this country will reach those found in Western Europe in the near future, given the emphasis upon the emotional meaning of marriage in the United States. For example, nearly 20% of all couples living together under "marriage-like" conditions in Sweden are unmarried, and most of the married population has engaged in premarital cohabitation at one time or another (Trost, 1981). The percentages for the Netherlands are somewhat lower than for Sweden, but trend studies predict that as many as 30% of all couples might be cohabiting by the year 2000. Nevertheless, as it becomes more apparent that AIDS also poses a threat to the heterosexual population, it is possible that even more individuals in the United States will elect to cohabit in order to obtain a steady sexual partner.

Attitudes in Society

Nonmarital cohabitation is rapidly losing its aura of being a criminal or even deviant lifestyle. Although incidents involving teachers and policemen being fired or suspended simply for living together with a girl- or boyfriend have taken place well into the 1980s, such occurrences are rare. Cohabitation in several U.S. states is still considered a felony, based on a legal code pertaining to "crimes against chastity," that goes back two hundred years, but these statues are seldom, if ever, enforced. Recent court decisions show a trend toward treating cohabiting couples in much the same way as married couples, with regard to division of common property and child visitation rights when a relationship is terminated.

College students have been found to be very positive towards nonmarital cohabitation arrangements, as long as they do not involve children. A study conducted by Donald Bower and Victor Christopherson (1977), using a large sample of students enrolled in family or marriage classes, revealed that some 60% favored cohabitation in order to try out a relationship, though more than 85% ruled out rearing children in an unmarried relationship. In general, students tend to be favorable toward cohabitation as long as the relationship is affectionate, somewhat egalitarian, monogamous, and child-free.

There are far more discrepant preferences in this respect among black men and women than among whites (Erickson, 1980; Rao and Rao, 1980). Black men are more in favor of cohabitation than black women. Despite reservations about cohabitation, many black women have little choice but to enter a cohabitational arrangement due to factors such as the shortage of black men and the need to obtain financial security.

Various surveys document increasing acceptance of nonmarital cohabitation among the general American public but also indicate that there is still considerable resistance to it. In a recent study (Wiersma, 1983), 72% of a United States sample of cohabiting couples reported that their relatives had reservations about their nonmarital relationship, and a similar percentage noted that their neighbors also felt this way. Several studies in the early 1970s found that the majority of students' parents would attempt to prevent their children from getting involved in such a relationship, or put a stop to it if it had already occurred.

Political scientists Herbert McClosky and Alida Brill (1983) report on a 1978/1979 *Time* survey in which it was found that 46% of the American public thought that living together unmarried was morally wrong (54% not morally wrong). The general public was even more negative toward such couples if children were involved (68% morally wrong; 32% not morally wrong).

Attitudes towards cohabitation are more positive in countries such as Sweden and the Netherlands, where cohabitation is well-integrated into society. In a comparative study, Geertje Wiersma (1983) discovered that the Dutch were indeed more accepting than the Americans, and that on several key questions there was a difference of approximately 15-20 percentage points. Various other studies in the Netherlands show that between 80% and 90% of the population approve of nonmarital cohabitation as a preparation for marriage, while less than 10% disapprove of it. A large majority (70%) of the Dutch population does not see any basic difference between cohabitation and marriage (Schelvis, 1983). But even in the Netherlands, only a small proportion of all cohabitors is as yet opposed in principle to marriage — 12% according to the study by Wiersma (1983). Many couples indicate that marriage is not likely but that it is a possibility, provided it would be beneficial in a practical sense (i.e., easier when children arrive). The same study shows that at this point in time only 12% of Dutch cohabitors (as opposed to 5% in the U.S.) would consider having a child while continuing to cohabit. Nevertheless, an increasing number of couples in the Netherlands elect to have children without getting married, often arranging legal matters in specially prepared contracts.

VARIETIES OF NONMARITAL COHABITATION

Besides the fact that all nonmarital cohabiting couples live in a joint household on a regular basis without being married, we can find an enormous diversity of lifestyle arrangements. We focus here particularly upon typologies that are based upon the attitudes of the participants towards their lifestyle. Even from this perspective, however, many typologies may be developed, depending upon the dimension that is emphasized.

Cees Straver (1981) elaborated a typology on the basis of a study of cohabitors from all social levels who were predominantly in their thirties. Thus, this study did not focus upon the student cohabitors who are the predominant subjects in most American studies. According to Straver, in contrast to married couples, unmarried partners are free to decide whether or not to fulfill all kinds of functions for each other. For example, they can decide whether or not to provide financial support for the other, whether or not to keep their finances completely separate, and whether or not to take responsibility for each other's children. The degree in which the couples emphasized togetherness and joint responsibility (versus autonomy and independence) with regard to such divergent issues as money, possessions, and friendships was indeed discovered to be an important dimension on which cohabiting couples varied. Among the types of relationships distinguished were the following:

1. *Traditional role pattern:* a sharp delineation of roles; the woman and children are economically dependent upon the man; the woman takes care of the household; both live in their own separate worlds, but feel responsible for one another.

2. *Complete togetherness:* these partners do much more together; they pool their finances; their possessions are jointly owned, and they expect their relationship to be permanent.

3. *Limited togetherness:* togetherness remains the guideline, especially with respect to finances, but the partners strive toward more independence and autonomy; they may visit friends alone, and sometimes have outside sexual relationships; permanency is preferred, but not at any cost.

4. *Independence:* the goal of the relationship is not to promote togetherness, but to promote self-fulfillment; there is a large degree of economic independence; and the partners will enter into a new relationship if it means more to them.

Straver's typology seems particularly relevant for older, more or less settled cohabitors, who may have been married before and have children in their household. However, it does not seem the most adequate classification for young cohabiting couples. With regard to this last category, the typology of Carl Ridley and his colleagues (1978) may be more useful. They distinguish four patterns of cohabital dynamics, that are based on the reasons for cohabiting:

1. *Linus Blanket:* one or both of the partners enter the relationship mainly out of dependency needs. The primary goal is to avoid loneliness and insecurity.

2. *Emancipation:* one or both partners enter the relationship to become independent and free themselves from parental constraints. The relationship is a kind of escape route.

3. *Convenience:* a rather temporary arrangement (handy for the moment) that serves to provide the partners with a regular sexual outlet and other advantages of having a stable partner. Fear of AIDS might lead to a large increase in this type of cohabitation.

4. *Testing:* a more or less conscious decision to live together in order to develop further and enrich a relationship.

The first three forms are not conducive toward promoting a stable, successful, and highly satisfying bond. Testing, on the other hand, is supposed to offer the highest potential for intimacy and durability.

Other typologies focus upon the role of cohabitation in one's pattern of durable relationships. In this respect, at least four different types of cohabitational relationships can be distinguished (Macklin, 1983; Lewis et al., 1977).

1. *Temporary or casual:* often pragmatic factors extrinsic to the relationship play a role; the partners are not committed to staying together.
2. *Going together:* the partners live together because they are emotionally involved, but have no clear plans for the future.
3. *Transitional, preparation for marriage:* cohabitation is primarily a stage between casual dating and marriage (Macklin, 1974), during which the couple develops the relationship and gets to know one another better.
4. *Alternative for, or escape from, marriage:* the couple opposes marriage for emotional, practical, or ideological reasons. Such a relationship could either be temporary or have a more permanent nature.

Almost all American cohabitors (various findings indicate that this is approximately 90%) plan to eventually marry, either to their present partner or someone else, although usually somewhat later in life than noncohabitors. Cohabitation can thus be considered premarital behavior in the context of a new courtship pattern, and marriage becomes a step towards firm commitment after the looser cohabitational lifestyle. In fact, there is evidence that cohabitation does not postpone the actual onset of marriage, and might even accelerate the decision to marry (Yamaguchi and Kandel, 1985). In a study conducted by Wiersma (1983, p. 88), 69% of her sample of cohabitors agreed with the statement "if the relationship is a good one, the next step is marriage." This strongly suggests that nonmarital cohabitation does not usually tend to be a permanent form of heterosexual union.

Finally, we must point to a type of cohabitation that is especially found among lower income blacks and is referred to as the "live-in boyfriend" arrangement (Sauer, 1981). Frequently, this arrangement comprises a divorced woman with children who shares a residence with a man who is separated from his wife. The boyfriend fulfills the role of supportive companion and provides for the sexual and intimate needs of the woman. In some cases, he supplies financial assistance, protection, or performs other useful functions, but his role remains of second-ary importance to the family unit. Both parties show little commitment to the relationship and there are few intentions to solidify and formalize it, making it highly vulnerable and fragile. In some cases, the boyfriend does not really live with the woman, but provides financial support, is involved in the socialization of the children, and is openly acknowl-edged by friends and kin (Cazenave, 1980).

CHARACTERISTICS OF COHABITORS

Some characteristics of cohabitors, in terms of age and marital status, were dealt with earlier. In this section we will focus upon some other features of cohabiting individuals. To begin with, we need to discuss some issues that have proven inherently problematic in studies on nonmarital cohabitation. An initial problem is that many of the earlier studies focused on college student populations, usually comparing students who had ever cohabited with those who had never done so. Since most cohabitors are not college students, it is difficult to draw definite conclusions from such studies. A second problem is that even in studies employing samples that are representative of the larger population, inferences are made with respect to the umbrella category "cohabitors" without specifying to what extent these conclusions hold for the various types of cohabiting relationships we distinguished ear-lier. It is rather likely that those who choose cohabitation as an alterna-tive to marriage are different from those for whom this lifestyle is a preparation for marriage or simply a convenient sexual arrangement. Finally, the choice of a comparison group is often problematic. In general, it makes most sense to compare the characteristics of those who cohabit to those who are similar in terms of age, educational back-ground, and marital status, but who, instead of cohabiting, opt for marriage or living in separate residences. However, many studies have not always done this, leading to faulty comparisons. Despite these qualifications, there are various characteristics that are consistently found in studies of individuals who have cohabited.

1) Religion. A recurrent finding in nearly all studies on cohabitation is that cohabitors are less religious than comparable others. This holds true whether one measures frequency of church attendance or religious commitment. In fact, there is an almost linear relationship between level of religiosity and likelihood of having cohabited. Clayton and Voss (1977), for example, asked their sample how often they attended church. Seven percent of those who attended on a weekly basis had cohabited; of those who attended monthly — 12%; less than monthly — 19%; never — 26%. This supports the common notion that religion has an inhibiting influence on nonmarital intimate and sexual behavior. In general, religious denomination has not been found to be a predisposing factor with respect to the likelihood to have cohabited, although sometimes Catholics or Jews have been found to be overrepresented among cohabitors.

2) Attitudes towards sexuality. Married couples who have cohabited are more experienced in the area of sexual behavior than those who have not cohabited. Initial intercourse among the first group occurred at an earlier age — on the average of two years earlier. According to the results of Clayton and Voss (1977), 48% of those who had cohabiting experience had engaged in intercourse by the age of fifteen, as opposed to 23% who had not cohabited. Cohabitors also report significantly more sexual partners, more diverse sexual activities, and more sexual experimentation. In a study of marrieds, cohabitors, gays, and lesbians, Philip Blumstein and Pepper Schwartz (1983) found that both male and female cohabitors were more favorable than their married counterparts toward sex without love, and were more tolerant of nonmonogamy. We shall return to the subject of sexuality later when relationship characteristics are discussed.

3) Lifestyle and political views. According to earlier research, co-habitors are more likely to be politically liberal and have more experience in all sorts of unconventional behavior. Typical unconventional behaviors that tended to differentiate cohabitors from noncohabitors are illicit drug use; interest in astrology, ESP, or Eastern religions; vegetarianism; "bumming around the United States or elsewhere" attending rock concerts or festivals; attraction to other alternative lifestyles, such as communes and law-breaking behavior. In general, cohabitors appeared less inclined to adhere to social norms. As cohabitation is gradually affecting a larger cross-section of society, the differences between those who have and those who have not engaged in this lifestyle are becoming smaller. Spanier (1983), who analyzed the 1980 census data on cohabitation, was somewhat surprised to discover an overt trend toward convergence between some of the social and economic characteristics of married and unmarried couples.

4) Personality. Research, generally based on student populations, points to existing personality differences. It conveys evidence of counter-traditional sex roles: women cohabitors have been found to be more assertive, independent, and managerial than their noncohabiting peers, whereas their male partners describe themselves as warmer, more emotionally dependent and supportive, less aggressive, and less managerial than other men. According to Michael Newcomb (1981), cohabitors tend to have fewer internalized constraints on their behavior, as is evidenced by being less religious, more androgynous, more liberal, and more sexually experimental.

5) *Family background.* There is evidence that those who cohabit instead of marry have a relatively unhappy family background. Compared with similar married couples, cohabitors are more likely to have parents who are divorced, to describe the marriage of their parents as unhappy, and to have poorer relationships with their parents (Wiersma, 1983; Newcomb, 1986; Tanfer, 1987). Wiersma, for example, found that 23% of the parents of cohabitors were divorced, versus not more than 1% of the parents of married subjects in her study. Of the latter, 58% also described the marriage of their parents as extraordinarily happy, while among the cohabitors only 40% did so.

In a recent study conducted by Newcomb (1986a), using a large sample of Los Angeles-based young adults who had initially been contacted in high school and subsequently followed for nine years, the majority of findings described above were replicated (though several were hardly identifiable and some novel ones were reported). Though this longitudinal study also examined differences between cohabitors (those who had ever cohabited) and noncohabitors in general (single, married, or living with parents), we shall concentrate on the differences Newcomb found between the first group and the marrieds who had not cohabited in the past. The only personality variable that actually differentiated male cohabitors from the marrieds was that they were reportedly more generous. On the other hand, cohabiting women differed from their married counterparts on a wide variety of variables. They tended to be less deliberate, less diligent, less law abiding, religiously less committed, less self-accepting, less independent, and less lonely after an argument. Furthermore, they were more inclined to enjoy doing things on their own. Interestingly, cohabiting women indicated to a much greater extent that their relationships with parents and family were severely strained, while this was not the case for men. This finding may indicate a high incidence of emancipatory motives on the part of women. However, it may also reflect that many parents of cohabitors still embrace the traditional cultural assumption that in unmarried unions it is the men who stand to benefit, while the women can easily be taken advantage of, and become the victim of a man's tendency to be promiscuous and avoid responsibility. The fact that cohabitors report that their parents are more negative toward sex than noncohabitors points in this direction (Newcomb, 1986b). When one's daughter chooses to cohabit in spite of parental resistance, this can be a source of intense familial conflict.

THE PUSHES AND PULLS OF COHABITATION

The Choice to Cohabit

Although couples may sometimes make a deliberate choice to live together after discussing all the pros and cons involved, this is not generally the case. For most couples it is even difficult to determine when they actually began to live together. In a study of students conducted by Eleanor Macklin (1974), no more than 25% of the students surveyed had discussed whether they would cohabit before they actually did so. Usually, a courtship pattern is set in motion by dating, which then leads to the partners spending increasing amounts of time together and gradually drifting into a cohabiting arrangement. At first, one night a week is spent together, then two, three, etc., until at a certain point a decision is made to move the personal possessions of one of the partners to the other's living quarters. Many cohabitors maintain their old living quarters in the initial stage of the relationship in case something goes wrong. Given the lack of explicit discussion, it is not surprising that for most couples the decision to live together is low key and involves few explicit commitments. Especially students do not, either consciously or unconsciously, have marriage in mind as a future outcome when they start living together, and are seldom committed to marrying the current partner or working hard to develop a lasting relationship.

In general, as is the case for other lifestyles, living together is the result of several pushes and pulls acting on the individual. Structural factors, such as lack of social control by the parents and relaxed regulations in the dormitories, clearly make cohabitation an attractive option for many young students. This is especially true since there is a general tendency among both young men and women in contemporary society to postpone marriage and the starting of a family, while expending considerable efforts to search for means of self-actualization, an independent identity, self-advancement (educationally and career-wise), and personal growth. On the other hand, there remains a desire for stability, security, and close relationships. In short, the young are caught in an ambivalent situation, with pushes and pulls in both the directions of independence and emotional involvement. Given these conflicting needs, cohabitation becomes an interesting option. It offers some advantages of singlehood, such as the opportunity to remain (at least partially) autonomous, independent, and basically uncommitted, as well as many advantages of marriage, such as the sharing of intimacy, sexuality, companionship, and affection (Newcomb, 1981). Cohabitation may actually be a lifestyle that allows young people to resolve the transitional problems between childhood and adulthood. Indeed, young cohabitors do not, for the most part, reject the institution of marriage (and family), but also do not consider themselves ripe for a marital union yet.

The nature of the situation in which divorced individuals find themselves differs considerably from that of young inexperienced college students (or other inexperienced young adults), and their motivations for cohabiting deviate correspondingly. They have been confronted with a marriage that has failed, and although they may still be interested in remarrying, past experience has taught them to be extra cautious in order to avoid another painful failure. Because children are sometimes involved, a successful, long lasting, and stable relationship is high on the scale of desirable items. In these instances, cohabitation is often more the result of a conscious and active decision to test the viability of a relationship.

The basic meaning and underlying motives for the black boyfriend arrangement are again of a different nature. The centrality of children that is prevalent here can be counterposed to the more existentially and personal growth-oriented relationships of affluent whites. A main reason for the black woman to become involved is emotional and financial support, and companionship. For the man the arrangement provides for a steady, intimate and sexual partner, without the burden of long-term responsibility associated with marriage. This is not to say that these motives are uncommon among affluent whites, as we have seen, but that they are more overtly and almost institutionally present in some black communities (Cazenave, 1980).

Negative Aspects of Cohabitation

Some problems are common to all types of cohabitation. A first problem concerns the ambivalent attitude toward commitment, security, attachment, togetherness, and dependence, on the one hand, and autonomy, freedom, independence, and personal growth, on the other. These can be the cause of serious problems and tension within a cohabiting relationship. All couples must agree to some kind of balance, but due to the transitional stage in life of many cohabitors, their search for a mutually satisfactory balance can constitute a pivotal and recurrent issue. Too much of an emphasis on togetherness can make one or both of the partners feel trapped or used; too much autonomy can make them experience a lack of belonging, a loss of security and/or loneliness. Wiersma (1983, p. 41) notes that in view of the anxieties of cohabiting individuals, as compared with married individuals, "reciprocity in the relationship, equality in sharing tasks, a sense of personal freedom, competitiveness and arguments with the partner are more often matters of concern and predicament."

It needs to be stated that the alternative for many couples — singlehood — is hardly perceived as attractive. Singlehood lacks precisely what so many believe is rewarding about cohabitation, companionship, emotional support, frequent and steady sexual opportunities, and a sense of belonging.

A problem of an entirely different nature also encountered by cohabiting couples deals with the consequences of the lack of legal (or, even, more informal) arrangements that protect the interests of both individuals. Ironically, although many couples are trying to avoid legal arrangements, i.e., marriage, they can later be confronted with the negative consequences of not having drawn up any legal provisions: problems pertaining to ownership of property, goods and money; visiting rights in case of illness or death; rental contracts, and leases; and responsibility for children. Very few couples ever make provisions for separation and, according to Straver (1981), bitter fights over such issues during separation appear to be the rule rather than the exception when unmarried couples split up.

From Cohabitation to Marriage

Although few couples elaborately discuss their decision to live together in advance, most cohabiting couples seem to spend a great deal of time discussing whether to marry or continue cohabiting. Two factors seem to affect the decision to get married: 1) the seeking of legitimacy and acceptance by society, especially with respect to children; and 2) the expression of love and commitment, as well as the longing for security (Kotkin, 1983). In the previously discussed study (Wiersma, 1983, p. 89), it was discovered that the second factor was more important for American cohabitors. For them, "marriage is very much the crown upon a successfully completed cohabitation period." They marry primarily to express their love and commitment and to seek stability and emotional security. Dutch cohabitors, however, viewed marriage more as a formality, a step that one could eventually decide to take, particularly if one wanted children or wanted to make use of the legal advantages associated with marriage. What the data from this project actually indicate is that Dutch cohabitation resembles Dutch marriage, while the two lifestyles in the United States differ much more from one another. The institution of marriage, as such, seems more highly valued in an emotional sense by Americans, while, in the Netherlands, cohabitation is more integrated within, and accepted by, society.

FEATURES OF THE COHABITING RELATIONSHIP

A cohabiting union is, in the first place, a close, intimate relationship, and as in other intimate relationships, the partners have to deal with such issues as commitment, division of tasks, communication, and sexuality. In general, such phenomena and processes in cohabiting relationships have not been studied in their own right, but almost always in comparison with married, dating, or engaged couples. As will become clear, cohabiting couples do indeed differ from other couples in several ways.

Sexual Behavior

Although findings from different studies have not been completely consistent, cohabiting couples tend to be sexually more active and have a higher level of sophistication and experimentation when compared to similar married couples. For example, Newcomb (1983) reanalyzed the data of several studies and found that cohabitors had a greater frequency of intercourse and orgasm with their partner, used more varied positions during coitus, and had higher levels of sexual communication than married couples. Nevertheless, sexual satisfaction was not higher among the cohabitors and, in one study (Blumstein and Schwartz, 1983), marrieds, gays, and lesbians were even found to be sexually more satisfied than cohabitors.

Considerable attention has been devoted to the issue of sexual relationships outside of the dyad. Though cohabitors do tend to be more supportive than marrieds or engaged couples of the idea that sexual freedom should be allowed in a relationship, they have been found to be primarily monogamous (some 70% of cohabiting couples report they are totally monogamous). Cohabitors engage more often in sexual intercourse outside the dyad than marrieds, and this is especially pronounced for cohabiting couples who consciously elect to remain unmar-

"I don't need marriage as an institution. But both of us will have professional careers, and if society is gonna feel happier about me being married . . . I don't want to be screwed out of a good consulting job because some 60 year old guy knows I'm not married and living with a woman and doesn't like it."

"I think you work harder to maintain your relationship if you're married. If your relationship starts to fall apart, and you're just living together, it's easier to say, "Let's split.' I'm not sure if this is a good think or bad. Sometimes a relationship should end. I don't think a relationship should persist at all costs."

Figure 3.2 Marriage versus cohabitation

Source: Kotkin (1985).

ried for an extended period of time (Blumstein and Schwartz, 1983). This indicates a certain hesitance to commit oneself totally to the partner. In the Netherlands, on the other hand, because of the different meaning of cohabitation, we see a different picture. In a study of 52 cohabiting and 198 married persons, it was found that about the same percentage (22%) had engaged in sex outside the relationship in both groups (Buunk, 1980a).

Cohabiting men seem to be more in favor of extrarelational sexual relationships than cohabiting women. Furthermore, one study showed that women in cohabiting relationships react with *more* jealousy to their partners' extradyadic sexual involvements than do married women. In contrast, there was no difference in the degree of jealousy between married and cohabiting men (Buunk, 1986). Probably, cohabiting women react so strongly to their partners' outside sexual relationships because their own relationship lacks solidity and commitment, therefore posing a greater threat to the relationship. Such a situation seems to bother men to a lesser degree.

Communication, Love and Satisfaction

The data on the quality of the relationships of cohabiting couples are somewhat contradictory. In general, early research did not show differences in the level of relational satisfaction and communication between married couples and those just living together but did indicate that, compared to dating couples, cohabiting couples reported more love, more mutual self-disclosure, and fewer problems in their relationship (Risman et al., 1981). Some recent research, however, provides a rather mixed picture. While a study by Newcomb (1986b) demonstrated that there are no differences between cohabitors and noncohabitors with respect to liking and loving one's partner, two other studies revealed that cohabiting couples scored lower in this area than married heterosexual, dating heterosexual, gay, and lesbian couples (Cunningham and Antill, 1981; Kurdek and Schmitt, 1986). Lawrence Kurdek and Patrick Schmitt (1986) explain that the low scores of the cohabitors in their study may have been due to two things: the fact that the cohabitors in the sample were together for a shorter time than the other types of couples, and also to a higher incidence of previous divorce among cohabitors, which makes them more cautious and "realistic" in their expectations of relationships.

Sex Roles

Cohabitors seem to attempt more often than marrieds to replace traditional sex roles with a more equal distribution of rights and responsibilities. Cohabiting couples are also much more prone than married couples to believe that both partners should work. Several studies show that despite such egalitarian attitudes there are few differences between cohabiting and married couples with respect to the performance of household tasks, the division of labor and decision-making power patterns. The man's duties in the household remain limited to minor chores such as repairs, yard work, cleaning up once in a while, and helping with the dishes. Generally speaking, though cohabiting women spend less time than wives doing housework, their partners do not spend more time than husbands doing this type of work. In one study (Stafford et al., 1977) that did show a less traditional division of labor in unmarried households, it became apparent that the ultimate *responsibility* for the tasks being performed matched the traditional value system. Slipping back into conventional sex roles is then quite easy. It is apparently easier to endorse egalitarian ideas and philosophize about them than it is to successfully put them into practice. It is therefore not surprising that cohabitors often have specific rules about sharing household chores and costs (Argyle and Henderson, 1985).

A related problem for women seeking an egalitarian relationship is the fact that the man's career is generally given first priority. There are numerous cultural pressures that favor and reinforce the man becoming involved in the race for status, salary, and success. Men's career demands may consequently force the women to adopt more traditional roles. Nevertheless, the focus on the man's career tends to be less explicit among cohabiting couples than married or engaged couples. In Mark Kotkin's (1983) sample of University of Pennsylvania student couples, he found that no less than 80% of married couples, 64% of engaged cohabiting couples, and 44% of nonengaged cohabiting couples had adopted attitudes and strategies favoring the man's career. This and other research indicates that the road to married life may eventually demand more sacrifices from the woman.

Commitment

Commitment is probably the variable that has been studied most extensively with regard to cohabitation. In general, cohabiting couples have been found to be less committed to their relationship than married couples. Illustrative are the data from Charles Cole's study (1977), which indicate that only a few of the cohabitors studied were committed to marrying their partner, or to definitely work hard to develop a lasting relationship. The majority wanted to stay together as long as the relationship was mutually satisfying or personally enjoyable. Only a minority entered into the relationship with the idea of making it permanent. This low commitment is, in fact, hardly surprising, especially for younger never-married cohabitors, who tend to start living together precisely because they do not yet want to commit themselves. One recent study reveals that about 6 out of 10 cohabitors break off their relationship before marriage (White, 1987).

Commitment is not a unitary concept but has several dimensions. Two components of commitment have been investigated in particular: 1) *personal* commitment, or the degree to which one will make efforts to continue the relationship, especially when difficulties arise; and 2) *behavioral* or *structural* commitment, i.e., the factors that bind one to the relationship, such as common possessions, combined finances, and being acknowledged as a couple by significant others (Macklin, 1983). As an illustration of the importance to distinguish between types of commitment, Robert Lewis et al. (1977) found that although cohabitors were less committed than the engaged to marry their partners, they did not differ in their degree of commitment to each other as such (called pair-bond commitment). Lewis and his colleagues point out that the stability of a relationship, as reflected in level of commitment, is related more to qualitative aspects for cohabitors (happiness, homogamy, dyadic consensus, and interaction), quantitative aspects for those engaged (length of acquaintance and mother's education), and a combination of both for married couples (couple happiness, length of acquaintance, and father's occupation).

Although the decision to cohabit can be related to a reluctance to become committed, it is precisely this lack of commitment that is often perceived as the major *dis*advantage of living-together arrangements once they become stabilized. As we suggested earlier, this seems to be particularly true for women. Indeed, in a study of singles, nearly half of the women and a third of the men acknowledged that they considered this a clear problem (Simenauer and Carroll, 1982). Macklin (1983) suggests that the relatively low degree of commitment established in American studies may not be found in Western Europe, where cohabitation is more of an integrated institution in society. Indeed, Wiersma's study (1983, p. 80) showed that American cohabitors seemed to be less committed in many ways, and less often resembled a "portrait of outward 'couple togetherness than Dutch cohabitors.'" This is also confirmed by the findings of Blumstein and Schwartz (1983) that cohabitors (especially the women) report a very strong need to have private time away from one's partner. Wiersma (1983) notes that when compared to their Dutch counterparts, American cohabitors had experienced other couple-relationships more frequently in the past, were more likely to be divorced, owned a house together less often, kept their finances and possessions separate much more often, and felt much more uncomfortable spending money earned by their partner. The American cohabitors had also made fewer provisions for separation and were more often subjected to social disapproval from parents, relatives, and neighbors. In all these respects, Dutch cohabitors were more committed to their relationship, and they themselves, as well as their environment, seemed to take the relationship more seriously. They were also more inclined to want their relationship to be a permanent one.

Stability

Cohabitation has repeatedly been shown to be a more unstable type of arrangement than marriage. Macklin (1983) concludes that 35% to 45% of U.S. couples who have lived together for six months eventually break up. Because cohabitation is often part of the courtship process, it is also worthwhile to compare cohabitation to the institution of dating. It appears that cohabitation and dating are quite similar in terms of dissolution rates. Among both college cohabitors and their dating counterparts, anywhere from 30% to 50% break up after two years or less (Risman et al., 1981).

Part of the reason for the relative instability of cohabitation as compared to marriage has to do with the trial character of this lifestyle and its concomitant lower levels of dedication and pair-bond commitment (this holds true especially for men). In addition, many of the legal and moral thresholds involved in getting divorced, and the external social pressures to keep a marriage going, are absent in nonmarital contexts. In fact, a comparison of heterosexual married, heterosexual cohabiting, and gay and lesbian relationships (Kurdek and Schmitt, 1986) showed that cohabiting couples reported the fewest barriers to dissolving the relationship. Unlike many marrieds who divorce, cohabitors who break up report that the quality of their relationship was actually quite reasonable, supporting the notion that they are more easily moved to dissolve their relationship. Another factor that may affect the stability of unions is the distance between the ideal of egalitarianism and the reality of the pervasiveness of traditional sex roles. This can prove to be unacceptable to modern "emancipated" women. Because men are, on the average, older than their partners and further advanced educationally or professionally, there often comes a time when a decision needs to be made that requires significant sacrifices from the woman. For women who value their independence, the act of accommodating to their partner's needs can be seen as an infringement upon their own individual desires with respect to education and work, and they may consequently leave the relationship.

Cohabitation has been found to be a more successful experience among those who were previously married than among those without marital experience. Newcomb (1986a) notes that young adults are too often still quite incapable of successfully negotiating such a lifestyle at a time in their lives when finding an acceptable balance between togetherness and autonomy can cause serious problems. The previously divorced are usually somewhat older than their inexperienced (college) counterparts and tend to have acquired more interpersonal skills.

To state that termination and separation might be easy for cohabiting partners would be an incorrect assessment of its effects. Mika and Bloom (1980) found that, in many respects, the termination of the relationship is as disruptive and painful for former cohabitors as it is for divorcé(e)s. Macklin (1983, pp. 64-65) suggests that the dynamics of breaking up among cohabitors:

> . . . are similar to those associated with divorce: denial, anger, grief, and gradual reintegration into single life, with the amount of stress experienced proportional to the degree of emotional involvement and the length of time together. Because there is less social stigma, less legal hassle, and usually less initial expectation of permanence, and cohabiting relationships are generally of shorter duration than marriage, there will probably be less guilt, less sense of failure, and a quicker adjustment to separation.

EFFECTS OF COHABITATION UPON MARRIAGE

With respect to the influence on a person's later marriage, proponents of cohabitation have argued that living together prior to marriage is an effective screening device and helps one to make the transition to married life. Poorly adjusted couples are weeded out, while other couples can get used to the day-to-day realities of married life, and can develop the interpersonal skills that are necessary for marriage. Research on this topic, however, does not always substantiate such optimistic expectations. In many studies, no differences have been found between the quality of marriages of couples who cohabited before their marriage and those who did not. Two recent studies even showed that marital communication, satisfaction, and adjustment was lower among married couples who had previously cohabited. This was particularly true for women (Watson, 1983; De Maris and Leslie, 1984). For some, individual disappointment with marriage may have occurred if marriage was seen as a way to resolve problems experienced while living together. For others, the basic expectations of what marriage would be like and how the relationship with one's partner would develop were causes of dissatisfaction. Alfred De Maris and Gerald Leslie (1984) suggest that cohabitation might not so much function as a filter, but might attract couples who, for whatever reasons, are less likely to report high levels of satisfaction when married. This might be related to a more critical attitude in general toward relationships and marriage, or to certain expectations of marriage that more conventional people do not have (e.g., egalitarianism and maintenance of a personal identity).

Although the above-mentioned findings apply to most types of cohabiting arrangements, they once again to not apply to the remarried. Among the remarried, several positive aspects have been found to be associated with having cohabited before remarrying. A study by Sharon Hanna and Patricia Knaub (1981) showed that the remarried who had cohabited scored higher on measures of family strength, marital satisfaction, and adjustment. These individuals also experienced more happiness, closeness, concern for the partner's welfare, environmental support, and positive commitment skills. It appears as if the remarrieds have the life experience to fully take advantage of the opportunities cohabitation provides. Paul Yelsma (1986) adds that age may also play a significant role. He discovered that there were few differences in verbal communication practices between married and cohabiting couples, but that irrespective of their marital status, older couples were better communicators, which was attributed to their maturity, experience, and more realistic attitudes.

As for the stability of marriages that are engaged in by former cohabitors, early studies showed that there were few, if any, differences in divorce rates between couples who had previously lived together and those who had not. However, more recent research indicates that the former are somewhat more prone to divorce. They are more inclined to have broken up, sought counselling and advice, and eventually become permanently separated or divorced (Newcomb, 1986a). It is possible that because cohabitors perceive fewer barriers to dissolve a relationship, they may carry such a perspective of things into their marriage, also lowering the threshold to separation here. Another important factor in this context might be the amount of time that couples allow to lapse before cohabiting. Studies reveal that marrieds wait considerably longer before getting married than cohabitors do before cohabiting (Wiersma, 1983). A shorter dating period also makes it more difficult to discover if the other is really a compatible partner. Interestingly, an exploratory study by Mark Rank (1981) clearly reveals that the longer individuals wait beforehand, the better the chances of a successful period of cohabitation and marriage. Those who first cohabited and then married (and were still married) took an average of 20 months before cohabiting and another 16 months before marrying. On the other hand, those who had gone through the process of cohabiting, marriage, and divorce had spent an average of 7.5 months dating before living together and another 14 months before marrying.

In closing, it is necessary to point out that caution should be exercised when interpreting the various differences that have been found between cohabitors and non-cohabitors. Many of the differences that surface in studies comparing cohabitors, steady daters, and married couples are not attributable to cohabitation as a lifestyle, but to the types of people who cohabit. As we indicated, they tend to differ from the average American with respect to family background, attitudes, political views, etc. Cultural environment is also a factor that can influence the results of studies. A recent study of a large sample of never-married Canadians, for instance, found the opposite relationship between marital stability and previous cohabitation (White, 1987). In the Canadian context, where the mean age of marriage is higher than in the United States, and where marriages tend to last longer and be more stable, cohabitation was positively related to later marital stability.

REVIEW QUESTIONS

1) Is cohabitation generally a substitute for marriage in the United States? Explain. What various types of attitudes towards marriage are found among cohabitors? What are generally their motivations to get married?

2) What conflicting desires do many cohabitors encounter in their relationship?

3) What does the evidence tell us about marital satisfaction when marriage takes place after cohabitation? Can you relate this to the characteristics of cohabitors and the various types of cohabiting relationships?

SUGGESTED PROJECTS

1) Make a list of all the advantages and disadvantages that you think are associated with nonmarital cohabitation. Discuss this in class.

2) Try to picture two scenarios: one in which cohabitation completely replaces marriage in society and one in which cohabitation disappears entirely and marriage resumes its traditional role. In order to do this, attempt to isolate as many relevant factors as possible that might influence the future of nonmarital cohabitation (political situation, laws, housing, work demands, beliefs, values, etc.). In which direction do you think we are headed?

3) Go to the library and find a recent journal on nonmarital cohabitation (use *Psychological Abstracts* or *Sociological Abstracts*). Read the article and write a summary of it, placing it in the context of what is discussed in this chapter (do this by focusing on the issues covered in the article and those that are not).

Gay and Lesbian Lifestyles and Relationships

DEFINING HOMOSEXUALITY

IN CONTRAST TO THE OTHER LIFESTYLES discussed in this book, we shall be discussing relationships between individuals of the same sex here, usually referred to as homosexual relationships. Homosexuals can be either men, often labelled "gays"; or women, labelled "lesbians."

Historically speaking, the term "homosexual" is a fairly recent invention. The term was probably first used around 1870 by the Hungarian physician K. M. Benkert and was incorporated into the English language a little over a decade later. Before that time, there were only words for homosexual *behavior,* such as "buggery" and "sodomy." However, the emergence of the term homosexual reflected the fact that homosexuality was increasingly perceived as an inner characteristic of a particular *type* of individual (Weeks, 1977; Conrad and Schneider, 1980).

For a long time, no distinction was made between male homosexuality and transvestism, the practice of wearing women's clothes. It is often still thought that a homosexual is someone who looks and acts like a member of the opposite sex, and that homosexuals can be distinguished on the basis of overt appearance and mannerisms. Dressing and acting like a member of the opposite sex are no indicators at all, however, of who is and who is not homosexual, so that this early definition of homosexuality was easily refuted. In reality, the overly effeminate male homosexual is viewed with some disdain by many gays, and in recent years the gay subculture has come to value what it considers to be the more masculine traits of men. According to Anne Peplau and Steven Gordon (1983, p. 227), much of the confusion surrounding homosexuality stems from a faulty assumption in North America that:

three components of human sexuality are inseparable. These components are *sexual orientation* (attraction to same-gender versus other-gender partners), *gender identity* (our belief that we are male or female) and *gender-role behavior* (acting in traditionally "masculine" or "feminine" ways).

What then constitutes a homosexual? Is this category to include everybody who has ever been involved in a homosexual sex act or only those that engage in these acts exclusively and lifelong? Are those individuals who are sexually attracted to members of the same gender but do not act upon these feelings to be considered homosexual? How about individuals who feel attracted to, and have sexual relations with, both genders? Should we restrict the homosexual label to those individuals who identify themselves as such? In sum, do we need to look at behavior, feelings, fantasies, interactions, ideas, societal labelling, self-perception, or a combination of these?

Although it would be possible to define homosexuals as those individuals involved in homosexual activities with a certain frequency, there are serious limitations to such a definition. First, there has to be an element of free choice and a preference for homosexual relationships, under conditions where heterosexual relationships are available. It has been shown that homosexual behavior is likely to occur in places where there is no access to the other gender, such as in prisons (Kirkham, 1971). As soon as this access is made possible again, many individuals immediately terminate their homosexual behavior and revert to past heterosexual behavior patterns. The overwhelming majority of inmates who have sex with other inmates would not consider themselves to be homosexual and would sharply reject any suggestion in that direction. On the other hand, there are those who have strong sexual desires exclusively for those of the same gender, but who for various reasons never have actually been involved in a homosexual relationship. Not to call such persons homosexuals would be a distortion of reality. A last objection to defining homosexuality on the basis of behavior is the focus on the purely sexual dimension of homosexuality, i.e., same-gender sexual conduct. Being homosexual involves much more than simply having sexual intercourse with someone else who happens to have the same type of reproductive organs. Most homosexuals look for emotionally meaningful relationships, notwithstanding the fact that many male homosexuals have multiple and casual sexual encounters.

Given the foregoing, a homosexual can be defined as: a person who prefers sexual interaction and intimate relationships with members of the same gender. With this definition we consciously move away from the often exclusive focus on the object of the sex act or sexual desires (Harry, 1983). This focus upon intimacy is all the more salient with respect to lesbian relationships in contemporary society. Sexual gratification tends to be less of a primary goal for lesbians than for many male homosexuals involved in the gay subculture. It has been well-documented for both gays and lesbians, however, that for many, the ultimate goal tends to be the maintenance of an intimate relationship with a partner of the same gender.

SOCIETAL CONTEXT

Incidence in Society

It is almost common knowledge that male homosexuality was practiced in antiquity and that the ancient Greeks placed a very high value upon certain types of homosexual relationships. Peter Conrad and Joseph Schneider (1980) note that homosexuality in Greece was only considered healthy when embedded in a generally approved social and spiritual context. Same-gender conduct for the sole reason of sexual gratification was rejected. With the gradual domination of the Roman Empire, and later of Christianity and Christian values in the Western world, homosexual behavioral expressions were discouraged and became taboo. Nevertheless, manifestations of male homosexuality have even been recorded throughout the repressive Middle Ages, when homosexual acts led to the burning at the stake of those involved. Due to severe penalties up until the twentieth century, homosexuality was conducted in secrecy. There was no overt subculture as it now exists.

Much less is known about the history of lesbian relations. In American novels of the past, for instance, one is hard pressed to find any mention of this phenomenon (Bell, 1971). Little information is available that would give us an idea about the prevalence of lesbian lifestyles until roughly the beginning of the twentieth century.

Although it is difficult to give an accurate figure of how many people are homosexual in contemporary America, or are engaged in a homosexual lifestyle, the findings of the large-scale surveys of Alfred Kinsey and his associates (1948, 1953) have given us a fair estimate of how many individuals have had sexual experiences with same-gender partners. It was discovered that 13% of all American women had experienced at least one homosexual contact to the point of orgasm. Another 15% had homosexual desires but had not given in to these. Only 2% of the female population, however, were exclusively homosexual in their activities (70% were exclusively heterosexual). For men these figures were even more pronounced: 37% to the point of orgasm, 13% with unfulfilled desires, 4% exclusively homosexual, and 46% exclusively heterosexual. These results succeeded in startling a great many Americans, but a later *Psychology Today* survey (Athanasiou, Rubinstein, and Shaver, 1972) found basically the same figures. Based on these findings, it would appear that there may be as many as five million men and two and one-half million women in present day America who have a predominantly homosexual orientation.

Although the majority of men and a substantial group of women have had homosexual experiences, these experiences are mostly restricted to adolescence and early adulthood, when there is a certain amount of sexual experimentation with same-gender partners. Kinsey's findings actually confirm what anthropology has taught us about sexuality. Clellan Ford and Frank Beach (1952), in a cross-cultural study of sexuality, pointed to the fact that the great majority of cultures recognize the existence of such behavior, especially in adolescence, and that most have an accepting attitude towards certain manifestations of it. In only a few cultures, however, do we find an actual *preference* for same-gender relations. It has been claimed that, in general, exclusive homosexuality only occurs in societies which, as American society does, define homosexuality and heterosexuality as mutually exclusive (Reiss, 1986). In numerous societies, we witness people engaging in both homosexual and heterosexual behavior at some point in their lives (Ford and Beach, 1952; Kottack, 1974). The Aranda of Australia, for instance, require males to be exclusively homosexual during adolescence and bisexual after marriage, and define themselves as bisexual. Some contemporary Arab societies regard homosexual desires as evidence of potential bisexuality. This is a recognized and tolerated aspect of society, while exclusive homosexuality is not.

What does the future hold in store? There is no reason to assume that the percentage of the male population that is exclusively gay will change in the foreseeable future. However, given the fear of AIDS among male homosexuals, those who have only engaged in such relationships or behavior sporadically, or have merely thought about ventures in this direction, will be hesitant to risk becoming involved in what has come to be seen as a high-risk activity. For women the situation is different. AIDS is hardly found among lesbians, and the increasing pervasiveness of feminist ideas in society and a more positive climate of opinion towards sexual experimentation might make more women aware of the possibility of same-gender relationships. There are indications that this is already taking place. In an English study, 20% of the women surveyed claimed to have had a sexual affair with another woman (She, 1986). This is somewhat surprising given the fact that the survey was aimed at a heterosexual audience.

Attitudes in Society

In the past, male homosexuality in the U.S. was considered to be a crime. The history of American laws on male homosexuality is closely connected to English common law with its strong religious overtones. Traditionally, all sexual behavior not confined to the marital partner and not solely intended for procreation purposes has been condemned as immoral — including premarital sex, masturbation, and adultery. Concern with marriage, family, and the regulation of male lust led to laws on homosexuality that were closely linked to laws regulating prostitution. Gradually, with the rise of the medical profession to a dominant position in the late nineteenth century, the concept of crime was partially replaced by that of pathology. Physicians who had dealt with patients involved in same-gender contact "proposed that it was the product of a hereditary predisposition, 'taint' or congenital 'degeneration' in the central nervous system" (Conrad and Schneider, 1980, p. 181). Physicians often testified as expert witnesses in courts of law and insisted that homosexuals needed therapy, not punishment. The psychiatric profession embraced a similar view until the early 1970s and has only recently officially acknowledged that homosexuality is not a psychological disorder.

Even today, many states still have laws prohibiting homosexual behavior despite the changed attitudes in the scientific community. Until fairly recently, for instance, one could receive life imprisonment for homosexual activity with a consenting other in Nevada. Laws in the various states tend to employ different terminology in referring to homosexual behavior: "crime against nature," "buggery," and especially "sodomy" are most commonly used. Sodomy laws still exist in two dozen states, but are rarely enforced (Fig. 4.1). Nevertheless, as recently as 1986 the U.S. Supreme Court upheld, by a 5 to 4 margin, a Georgia law that makes it a felony for consenting adults to commit sodomy. The Supreme Court's decision was the first detailed decision on homosexual rights since it decided in 1967 to uphold a law, which still stands, refusing the entry of foreign homosexuals into the country. Furthermore, courts have been very reluctant, for instance, to grant child custody or sometimes even visiting rights to gay or lesbian parents. One study found that lesbian mothers win only about 15% of contested child custody cases (Hitchens, 1980).

How the States Regulate Sex

A movement to decriminalize sodomy began in 1961, joined eventually by 26 states. Two dozen states, mostly in the South and West, still restrict such behavior.

STATES WITH SODOMY LAWS	MAXIMUM JAIL SENTENCES FOR SODOMY	STATES WITH SODOMY LAWS	MAXIMUM JAIL SENTENCES FOR SODOMY
Alabama	1 year	Mississippi	10 years
Arizona	30 days	Missouri	1 year
Arkansas	1 year*	Montana	10 years*
Florida	60 days	Nevada	6 years*
Georgia	20 years	North Carolina	10 years
Idaho	5-year minimum	Oklahoma	10 years
Kansas	6 months*	Rhode Island	20 years
Kentucky	12 months	South Carolina	5 years
Louisiana	5 years	Tennessee	15 years*
Maryland	10 years	Texas	$200 fine*
Michigan	15 years (anal sex)	Utah	6 months
	5 years (oral sex)	Virginia	5 years
Minnesota	1 year	D.C.	10 years

*FOR HOMOSEXUAL SODOMY ONLY

Figure 4.1 Legal regulation of homosexual behavior

Source: Newsweek, July 14, 1986.

It must be noted, however, that legal discrimination against lesbians is a fairly recent development. In the past, lesbianism, unlike male homosexuality, was not illegal in most countries. In the U.S., Kinsey, Pomeroy, Martin, and Gebhard (1953) noted that from 1696 to 1952 there was not a single case on record of a sustained conviction of a woman for homosexual activities. In general, female homosexuality is considered to be less of a social problem than male homosexuality. Lesbian relationships do not so much elicit strong negative feelings among the general public but an ambiguous, almost puzzled reaction. One reason for the more severe response to male homosexuality may be that men and men's behavior tend to be valued more in Western society. Men are also more likely to be held responsible for their norm transgressions. Women are often viewed as being carried away by their emotions, or deceived in their innocence. Deviant male behavior is, therefore, considered to be more serious and more threatening to society, justifying the meting out of more severe punishment.

The legal situation largely parallels the general public's current attitudes. In the 1960s, along with the general increase of tolerance and loosening of norms, the American public became more tolerant of homosexuals and their relationships. Nevertheless, considerable resistance still exists. For example, as recently as 1986, 60% of the population were of the opinion that homosexuals should not be hired as elementary school teachers (Gallup, 1986). Although several surveys have found that 7 out of 10 Americans think that homosexual relations in private should be left up to the individual, an even larger majority of 78% considers such relationships to be morally wrong (Harris and Westin, 1979; McClosky and Brill, 1983). These findings indicate that sexual relationships between persons of the same gender may be *tolerated,* but that they are generally not *accepted* in the U.S. Many stereotypes and a high level of ignorance concerning homosexuals continue to exist. In general, homosexuals are still considered to be feminine and maladjusted; and no less than 42% of the population thinks that homosexuals should be understood as people who need help (McClosky and Brill, 1983).

Men and women differ in their tolerance of homosexuals. On the whole individuals tend to be *less* tolerant of homosexuals of their *own* gender. Thus, although women tend to endorse less traditional gender-role beliefs and are accordingly more tolerant of homosexuality in general (and gays in particular), they are less tolerant of lesbians than men are (Whitley, 1987).

As a consequence of a negative climate of opinion, institutional discrimination, especially of gays, has been pervasive in the areas of housing, employment, and the armed forces (though laws were passed in early 1988 to reduce discrimination here). The U.S. government has long enforced a policy of not hiring homosexuals because they presumably pose a security risk. It was reasoned that homosexuals can be easily blackmailed by parties who threaten to expose the person's lifestyle, a line of reasoning that tends to "blame the victim."

According to a recent Gallup survey (1986), the AIDS crisis has made individuals in the U.S. even *less* accepting of homosexuals (37% of those interviewed indicated that their opinions had become less favorable; 2% more favorable). On the question of legalization of homosexuality, the percentage favoring legalization remained stable (44%), but many who had previously answered "no opinion" now voiced their reservations toward legalization (1982: 39% opposed to legalization, 16% no opinion; 1985: 47% opposed to legalization, 9% no opinion). In other surveys, the public has claimed to be increasingly avoiding people they know or suspect to be homosexual. The lack of sympathy for the plight of gays in the midst of the AIDS threat is highlighted by a 1985 nationwide survey conducted by the *Los Angeles Times* (December 20, 1985). A full 28% of those surveyed stated that they believed that AIDS is God's punishment for homosexuals, while 23% stated that AIDS victims deserved what they were getting. Gay bashing is also on the rise. Between April and September 1984, and the same period in 1985, there was an 89% increase in violence against gays in San Francisco, while in New York this was even higher — 100%.

It is interesting to contrast American findings with other Western countries where attitudes are remarkably different. Homosexuality is much more easily accepted in Denmark and the Netherlands, for example. When the Dutch population was asked if they thought homosexuals should be allowed as much as possible to live in the way they deemed fit, 83.3% of all respondents answered in the affirmative (Middendorp, 1975). Another study in the Netherlands, conducted in 1981, showed that 63% of those interviewed considered homosexuality to be a normal type of behavior (28% considered it to be abnormal), and 87% thought that no restrictions should be placed on such behavior (9% were of the opinion that prohibitory actions should be taken) (De Groot and Visser, 1984). As far back as 1911, the Dutch government passed a law legalizing homosexual relations between consenting adults, and in 1971 the laws pertaining to homosexual and heterosexual relations were synchronized. Since 1971, sexual relations between consenting individuals are not illegal in the Netherlands if the parties involved are above 16 years of age.

It must nevertheless be noted that Western Europe also has a sad record in this century as far as discrimination against homosexuals is concerned: a little known fact is that homosexuals in Nazi Germany had to wear a pink triangle, and that 250,000 persons died in concentration camps because of their alleged homosexuality. More recently, in the wake of the AIDS crisis, the British government has taken steps that strongly discriminate against homosexuals. In early 1988, a new law was passed in Britain that makes it unlawful to promote homosexuality as a normal expression of sexuality. This means that teachers can be prohibited from telling their students that homosexual relations are acceptable, or an alternative to heterosexual relations; that local authorities are not to publish pro-homosexual information, or financially subsidize or otherwise support homosexual activities. All of this is easier to accomplish in Britain because, in contrast to the United States, this country has no written constitution with provisions concerning fundamental rights and freedoms.

VARIETIES OF HOMOSEXUAL LIFESTYLES

There is a tremendous variety in the intimate lifestyles of homosexuals. In fact, all lifestyles discussed in this book, and the varieties within those lifestyles, can be found among homosexuals. Thus, some homosexuals are married to someone of the opposite gender and have occasional homosexual affairs; others live alone, either being celibate or engaging in casual sex. Interestingly, young homosexuals have been found to be more in favor of communal arrangements than young heterosexuals (Sanders, 1977). In addition, there are many homosexuals who cohabit, sometimes in monogamous, sometimes in "open" relationships. In fact, all of the diverse types of unmarried cohabitation relationships mentioned in the last chapter, varying from the traditional role pattern to complete independence, were discovered in a study that included heterosexual as well as homosexual cohabiting couples (Straver, 1981).

As we indicated earlier, it is important to separate the lifestyle patterns of lesbians and gays. Due to a historically different societal reaction to male and female homosexuality, and differences with respect to socialization experiences, values, expectations, emancipation, and liberation ideologies, lesbian lifestyle patterns and experiences often take on an entirely different form from that of gays, and largely take place in a different type of subculture. We will therefore discuss lesbian and gay intimate lifestyles separately.

Lesbians

Lesbianism has been, and still is, much less visible than male homosexuality. Until fairly recently, when women became better able to support themselves financially, it was almost always economically infeasible for women to commit themselves to a lesbian lifestyle: there was just no way they could afford it. When the women's movement began to make headway in the early 1900s, the issue of lesbianism was discussed, but there was still extreme hesitation to acknowledge the existence of this type of relationship. In England in 1921, for instance, a proposal to make lesbianism punishable by law was defeated because people were afraid to attract attention to the phenomenon. As Lord Desart, a member of Parliament put it: "You are going to tell the whole world that there is such an offense, to bring it to the notice of women who have never heard of it, never thought of it, never dreamed of it. I think that is a very great mischief" (Weeks, 1977, pp. 106-107).

Sidney Abbott and Barbara Love (1978, p. 13) point out rather tongue-in-cheek that even today "the lesbian is one of the least known members of our culture. Less is known about her — and less accurately — than about the Newfoundland dog." The lack of a distinct subculture in the past is one of the major reasons that lesbian relationships have remained out of the public eye for so long. Another reason is that overt affectional exchanges between women are more culturally accepted than between men and will not be as rapidly labeled as homosexual-like behavior when observed by third parties. Whereas lesbian relationships in earlier times were carried on secretly between pairs of lovers or between members of a circle of friends, these relationships are now engaged in more freely.

Many lesbians, more than gays, are primarily interested in entering relatively permanent monogamous relationships. Some studies suggest that the average duration of such a relationship is somewhere between two and three years, but as the focus of most studies concerns young people, the actual average length is probably considerably longer. Nevertheless, many lesbian women find themselves going from one intimate and monogamous relationship to the next. In this regard, Joseph Harry (1983) speaks of lesbian relationship patterns as "serial monogamy." In accordance with this, there appears to be little need for a sexual relationship outside of one's primary relationship (Peplau et al., 1978). Because approximately one-third of lesbians living together were once married, and because there is often a desire to have children, many lesbian households include children.

One salient problem that confronts lesbian relationships is the attempt to attain, in practice, the equal balance of power that lesbians strongly endorse. Due to factors such as personal resources, experience, educational level, and varying interests it is not uncommon for one partner to assume more power. Mayta Caldwell and Anne Peplau (1984) note that despite the fact that almost 100% of their sample of lesbians from Los Angeles supported the idea of equal power, 40% of these women perceived their current relationship to be basically unequal. The results of this empirical study also clearly showed that inequality is related to dissatisfaction with the relationship.

In addition to finding an equal balance of power, there are other problems facing lesbian relationships. In a study of attachment and autonomy in lesbian couples (Peplau et al., 1978), germane relationship problems proved to be those dealing with independence, living too far apart, jealousy, differences in interests, and conflicting attitudes about sex (in the above order). Active feminists were found to reject culturally prescribed female roles, and valued personal autonomy more than those oriented towards dyadic attachment. They were less inclined to have strong commitment norms. Nevertheless, the majority of women in both of these studies indicated that there was considerable closeness and a high degree of satisfaction in their relationship. Another study, comparing married couples, nonmarried heterosexual couples, and homosexual couples (both lesbian and gay), showed that there were very few differences with respect to various indicators of satisfaction among the three groups (Kurdeck and Schmitt, 1986). Thus, the relatively short duration of lesbian relationships, compared to married couples, is not related to the degree of satisfaction the partners experience in the relationship, but probably to personal norms concerning commitment and external pressures to either stay together or break up. One structural element that can be found in lesbian relationships and can hasten the termination process is the frequent lack of stabilizing influences, such as social support, economic security, and status. In these respects, lesbian relations are comparable to many heterosexual cohabiting relationships.

One common belief is that in lesbian relationships one woman is masculine and assumes the husband's role (*butch*), while the other woman is feminine and assumes the wife's role (*femme*). The evidence tends to show that there is little or no truth to this assumption (Caldwell and Peplau, 1984; Lynch and Reilly, 1985/1986). In most cases there is no fixed division of roles and, much more so than in heterosexual marriages, there tends to be an emphasis on an egalitarian relationship. This applies to the sexual as well as domestic, social, and economic domains.

Although social networks of lesbian friends and acquaintances have existed since the early 1900s, and continue to be important, the advent of women's liberation and feminism has facilitated the emergence of a distinct lesbian subculture, comprised of numerous lesbian communities. There are now multiple coffee houses, theaters, bars, and businesses that cater to the needs of lesbian women and give them the opportunity to socialize openly.

The introduction of feminist theorizing into lesbian circles has altered some behavioral patterns of the past and facilitated the burgeoning of a wider diversity of lifestyle arrangements. Feminism has encouraged the development of personal autonomy, and there has been some increase in promiscuity among lesbians. Feminist theory also provides women with an overarching framework that justifies their choice for a female partner. The more radical exponents of such theorizing, which have gained a certain amount of support, consider men the enemy of women and advocate separatism (Wolf, 1979). There are even so-called "political lesbians," or "new gay" lesbians, who engage in lesbian relationships out of feminist solidarity with lesbians, out of a disenchantment with their male sexual partners, and what they perceive to be a suppressive male social order. "New gay" lesbians, thus, elect to define themselves as lesbian more out of political than sexual motives.

Gays

In contrast to lesbians, the subculture of gays is highly visible and has been the subject of a myriad of newspaper articles, local ordinances, public debates, and scientific articles. There is a strong urban flavor to the gay subculture, and it is especially well-established in San Francisco, New York, Los Angeles, and Miami. Robert Bell (1971) notes that these four cities account for approximately 60% of the entire gay scene in the U.S. Included in the subculture is an entire network of variant institutions, organizations, and businesses that cater to the gay's needs. Among these are magazines, doctors, lawyers, restaurants, bars, and baths. It is through this network that a gay community has been pieced together in various major cities. Many men organize their entire lives in line with the gay community (friendships, social affairs, work, leisure time), and their social identity is strongly influenced by its existence.

Gays involved in the subculture tend to be far more promiscuous than their lesbian counterparts or heterosexuals. Sex is often engaged in as a recreational activity, usually detached from any emotional involvement. One study found that while white male heterosexuals tend to have between five and nine sexual partners in their lifetime, the average white male homosexual tends to have close to a thousand (Bell and Weinberg, 1978). Approximately 60% of these liaisons are one-night stands or even more anonymous sexual experiences (Gagnon and Simon, 1973). Related to the focus on sexual gratification is a strong emphasis on physical appearance and youthfulness. However, the fear of AIDS has certainly led to a more cautious attitude toward casual sex.

The main public center in the gay community is the gay bar, which serves several functions. It provides an opportunity to meet and socialize with other gays in a sociable way, but more important is the fact that it enables "cruising" for sexual partners to take place. Lesbian bars fulfill this function far less. The bar scene is quite diverse, reflecting the large diversity of subcultures within the homosexual community. Some bars cater exclusively to the sadist and masochist population, the leather men, etc. The reason the bar has become such a focal point of the community may be that a place was needed that could be quickly closed and reopened in case of legal and police action against gay establishments, not only against bars but also against nightclubs, bath-houses, and other meeting places.

Some sexual encounters take place in certain designated public restrooms, sometimes referred to as "tearooms," which provide almost total anonymity and an almost complete lack of a relationship element. Laud Humphreys (1970) discovered that the crowd that frequents these restrooms does not usually frequent the bars. Instead, these individuals often have not publicly admitted their homosexuality and are still married (54%), or are otherwise isolated and lonely. The anonymity of the restroom, where sometimes not a word is exchanged, guarantees sexual gratification without running the risk of being exposed. Rest-room sex seems mainly an instrument for sexual release, an activity that is less lonely than masturbation but less involved than a relationship.

The number of male homosexuals that are part of the gay subculture represents a minority of the total gay population. And even among those who belong to the subculture, quite a few do not frequent bars or other establishments because they dislike their sexually predatory and phys-ically competitive nature. It has been reported that only about 5% of gays in San Francisco regularly attend the bathhouses. Even more noteworthy is the fact that a considerable number of homosexuals still lead an isolated existence and have never even been sexually involved with anyone. For example, Jacqueline Simenauer and David Carroll (1982) found that twice as many homo- and bisexual singles (10%) as heterosexual singles (5%) had never had a sexual partner.

Another fact about gays that is not well-known is that approximately 40% to 50% of them live within the context of a long-term relationship. Relatively more couples are found among gays in their twenties than among either younger or older gays (Harry, 1983), while the average length of a steady gay relationship is similar to that of lesbians, two to three years (Peplau and Amaro, 1982). Among men, however, there is a greater lapse of time between longer-lasting relationships than among women. The degree of satisfaction and love found in such couples is similar to that in marital couples (Kurdeck and Schmitt, 1986).

As we pointed out with respect to cohabiting heterosexual couples, the fact that such relationships tend to last shorter than marital unions is primarily due to a lack of barriers that make breaking up difficult. The marital bond, in itself, due to its almost sacred character in society, and the internalization of concomitant norms by the partners, puts more pressure on the couple to stay together. Vested interests by family (membership of a new family, family status, reputation, grandchildren, etc.) provide additional incentives not to divorce. Anne Peplau and Susan Cochran (1987) list several other important barriers that exist to a greater extent for marital couples: cost of divorce, spouse's financial dependence on the partner, joint property investments, and the presence of children.

As is the case for lesbians, there also exists a popular view that in gay relationships one male adopts the wife's role and the other the husband's role. Yet, again, the evidence does not bear this out. It is rare for one partner to be a houseperson. Most couples are dual-worker, dual-career units that share the household tasks. In only a small minority of instances does specialization in gender-type tasks occur. However, a certain type of imbalance is found more in gay than in heterosexual couples — the age difference between partners tends to be greater.

Increasingly, both gay and lesbian couples are drawing up contracts, wills, and powers of attorney in case one of the partners dies, becomes ill, or the couple breaks up. This is often done in religious services known as "gay unions." The services generally include a ritual resembling the marriage ceremony, and symbols of faith, such as the wearing of wedding rings, are used. In cases of illness or death where no contracts are drawn up, one partner can find him or herself barred from hospital rooms or thrown out of their own house because it was only registered in the other person's name.

An important issue in gay relationships is to find a way of dealing with extra-dyadic relationships. Total sexual exclusivity is very rare in gay relationships that have continued for several years, due to the traditional subculture emphasis upon sexual experimentation and sexual release. Understandably, then, a major problem in keeping gay relationships intact, besides the existence of external pressures, is the solving of the so-called "monogamy issue." Gay couples indicate that they place relatively little importance on monogamy (Blumstein and Schwartz, 1983). Correspondingly, some 4 out of 5 gays in a relationship claim to have had sex with someone other than their primary partner since the relationship started. For married couples, cohabiting heterosexual couples, and lesbian couples this is less than 1 out of 3. Agreement of both partners on this issue is not a guarantee of success or longevity, but it provides a more solid base for consensus on the type of lifestyle each partner wants to lead. The problems that can be encountered in this area are comparable to those found in sexually open marriages and will be discussed in more detail in Chapter 5. Suffice it to say here that a variety of factors are important for gay couples when deciding to adhere to an exclusive or nonexclusive lifestyle. David Blasband and Anne Peplau (1985) found that the most important factors that needed to be weighed in such a decision were personal attitudes toward exclusivity, needs for sexual variety, concerns about independence, and jealousy.

It has been suggested that many gays start out in a sexually exclusive relationship, but that as the relationship develops a shift towards non-exclusivity takes place, partially as a consequence of pressures from the gay community. Recent evidence does not bear this out (Blasband and Peplau, 1985). Furthermore, with the ubiquitous threat of AIDS in the late 1980s, we may be witnessing a process in which the number of gays committed to a single partner is steadily rising. The gay subculture's recent reassessment of the virtues of monogamy suggests that lengthy pair-relationships will be more commonplace in the future.

CHARACTERISTICS OF HOMOSEXUALS

Existing evidence on the most relevant demographic and social-psychological characteristics of lesbians and gays permits us to be very brief in our discussion. Contrary to common belief, homosexuality cuts across all boundaries of class, age, race, occupation, region, and religion. There is a greater tendency, however, for young, upper middle class, and higher educated homosexuals to enter the lesbian or gay subculture. Multiple psychological studies have attempted to uncover psychological differences between homosexuals and heterosexuals. With the exception of sexual orientation, homosexuals were consistently found to be indistinguishable from heterosexuals. In one study (Sanders, 1977), the results of 18 other studies into the differences in psychological functioning of heterosexuals and homosexuals were reviewed. The studies spanned the years 1957 to 1971 and employed a variety of psychological techniques. In total, 15 out of the 18 studies revealed *no* observable differences. Some of the differences that have been found in certain studies, such as the existence of more guilt, less self-esteem, and more stress among homosexuals, are not so much the result of personality differences, but can generally be attributed to societal rejection and a person's inability to cope with this. On the other hand, gays and lesbians tend to be more androgynous than heterosexuals, more egalitarian in their attitudes towards relationships, and strive for more of an equal power balance with their partner. These couples are far more inclined than married heterosexual couples, for instance, as are cohabiting heterosexual couples, to favor an arrangement in which both people work. The striving for equality in power, however, seems to be especially salient in lesbian relationships (Blumstein and Schwartz, 1983; Kurdek and Schmitt, 1986).

BECOMING HOMOSEXUAL: CAUSES AND MOTIVATIONS

Different types of factors affect the choice of a homosexual lifestyle than in the case of, for example, singlehood, extramarital relationships, and nonmarital cohabitation. Becoming homosexual is less of a free choice than these lifestyles, and external structural factors play a less important role. The often strongly felt emotional and sexual attraction to people of the same gender tends to be of overriding importance in opting for a homosexual lifestyle. Nevertheless, our knowledge is still inconclusive as to why one person becomes heterosexual and the other homosexual. During the Middle Ages it was believed that homosexuality was caused by the devil. It was repudiated as sinful and evil, often resulting in the execution of those suspected. Later, homosexuality was perceived as a form of moral degeneracy or gender confusion. These models are no longer given serious consideration, at least not in social-scientific circles where several different types of explanatory types of models have been presented. We summarize the most important below.

1) Biological and Genetic. Biological and genetic modes view homosexuality as the result of hereditary processes or hormonal imbalances, and tend to focus strictly on the expression of sexual behavior (instead of sexual relationships). Early biological theories of homosexuality posited that homosexuality was inborn and inescapable. Because of certain internal characteristics of certain individuals, it was assumed that one was destined to become either homosexual or heterosexual. In line with a renewed emphasis on genetic and physiological explanations, partially due to the rise of sociobiology in recent years (in which Darwinistic insights are used to explain social behavior), Lee Ellis and Ashley Ames (1987) argue, in a review of the literature, that homosexuality is the result of hormonal and neurological factors that operate during gestation. Especially critical, in their view, is how the brain responds to sex hormone infiltration between the second and sixth month of fetal development. These authors refer to, and base themselves heavily upon, mechanisms that led to homosexual behavior in other mammalian species. Other recent biological approaches to homosexuality focus on biological potential. Some individuals are considered to be more predisposed toward homosexuality because of biological factors, but one's environment can later influence the development of sexual orientation.

2) Psychoanalytic. Psychoanalytic models of the past have located the roots of homosexuality in psychological disturbances caused by a defective personality development. The only relevant outside influences in psychoanalytic models are usually the father and mother figures in a person's (early) childhood experiences. Due to a domineering, suffocating mother, and a weak, detached, rejecting, or absent father (and otherwise pathological familial interactions), it was assumed that a host of disorders could develop that were fertile soil for the development of homosexual tendencies: oral fixation, castration anxiety, fear of the opposite gender, flight from masculinity, etc. (the focus here is almost exclusively on male sexual development). Seduction was also seen as a precipitating factor in the onset of homosexuality. Research has generally failed to show that such factors play an important role in the development of homosexuality. A cross-cultural study by Frederick Whitam and Michael Zent (1984), for instance, based on interviews with American, Guatemalan, Brazilian, and Filipino male homosexuals, reveals that the link between family experiences and later homosexuality is, in part, due to cultural factors. The commonly held assumption that a domineering mother and a detached father are linked to homosexuality was only found to carry some truth in the United States. The authors suggest that American fathers may become detached and aggressive because they cannot accept their son's early cross-gender, effeminate behavior (e.g., doll-playing, cross-dressing, play preference for girls), something that was found to be indicative of later homosexuality in all four societies (cf Green, 1987).

3) Social Learning. Social learning models view one's homosexuality within a behavioristic framework. In simple terms, homosexual behavior is perceived to be the consequence of being rewarded for homosexual-related responses to stimuli in the environment, and punished for other types of responses. Another version of this model emphasizes the impact of children's imitations of adult homosexual behavior. Severe doubts have been voiced with respect to this approach. For example, several studies show that children growing up in gay or lesbian households do not have a greater inclination to become homosexuals themselves (e.g., Green et al., 1986; Hoffer, 1981). There is, however, some support for the so-called "learning through experience" model of adult sexual orientation, which stresses the sexual interaction with same-gender and cross-gender peers. An extensive study by Paul Van Wijk and Christiaan Geist (1984), for instance, suggests that early sexual arousal and experimentation involving others of the same gender increase the chances that a person will be homosexual in adulthood.

4) Oppression. A model that relates solely to female homosexuality, and that has gained a foothold among feminists, is the oppression model. The manifestation of lesbianism is framed within the context of women's protest against their gender's subordination in a patriarchal society. It is thus the extant social and political conditions, and the concomitant unequal state of male-female relations, that are responsible for women becoming lesbian. This ideological model has until now not been subjected to serious research efforts.

5) Identity Construct. The central tenet of the identity-construct model is that homosexuality is the result of a dynamic interplay between the individual and his or her social environment. There is a focus on the process of identity construction throughout life and how one comes to identify oneself as homosexual. The line of reasoning is as follows: based on one's early sexual desires and experiences, one uses the prevailing cultural definitions of behavior for identity purposes. Because homosexuality and heterosexuality are defined as mutually exclusive in Western society, one will be prone to perceive oneself as exclusively homosexual if one has had homosexual experiences or desires. Next, being labelled as homosexual by others (family, friends, peers) reinforces this self-definition. According to this model, the existence of early childhood desires is mainly used as explanatory legitimations and rationalizations for one's homosexuality at a later age. However, according to other identity construct models, a latent homosexual preference is already present in early childhood and becomes manifest later on. One interesting synthesis of several models is provided by Kenneth Plummer (1981). He claims that homosexual desires and experiences in childhood can serve to restrict the range of sexual preferences later on, and that adolescent and adult experiences help mold and further limit this childhood base.

The Development of Homosexuality

There are wide individual differences in the moment homosexual desires first arise. Homosexual feelings may surface early in life, but there have been many cases where persons did not become aware of their homosexual tendencies until they were far into adulthood, sometimes even into their fifties or sixties. One study of young homosexuals revealed the median age that women first discovered a feeling of attraction toward another woman was at 16 years, while the median age for full awareness was 18. For men these ages were 13 and 15, respectively (Sanders, 1977). On the average, there was a six-year lag for women between same-gender attraction and same-gender sexual behavior. For their male counterparts this was two years. The main reason for this discrepancy is considered to be the general cultural emphasis for men upon sexuality and women upon emotional attachment.

Men and women may employ different excusatory strategies in dealing with their first homosexual experiences. Women more often avoid perceiving themselves as lesbian by emphasizing their feelings, men by denying them. A woman will tend to rationalize a first homosexual encounter by referring to her love for that one particular person, rather than by acknowledging her lesbian feelings. A man, on the other hand, is more likely to deny responsibility (e.g., drunkenness), or refer to financial gain or sexual gratification as the reason for engaging in homosexual behavior. Again, there is an effort not to label oneself as homosexual. Continued homosexual activities may even lead to marriage because of the assumption that marriage will help one "go straight."

Various stage models have recently been advanced that attempt to trace the processes that take place before one does assume a homosexual identity and lifestyle (Cass, 1984; Chapman and Brannock, 1987; Minton and McDonald, 1983/1984). These interactional models show how initial homosexual feelings and fantasies set a gradual process in motion that eventually leads to the adoption of a homosexual identity. Both gays and lesbians (though there are some differences between them) tend to report that critical experiences and feelings in this process can include (though not necessarily in this order): initial same-gender feelings; fantasies or experiences; discovery that one is different from one's peers; self-questioning and confusion; negative feelings of guilt and shame; experimentation with sexuality and relationships; critically assessing the naturalness of heterosexuality and other societal norms; contacts with other homosexuals; self-disclosure of one's sexual orientation to heterosexuals (including family and friends); recognition and acceptance of one's homosexuality; adoption of a homosexual identity and lifestyle; and contact with a homosexual subculture.

For most homosexuals, the most significant event in the course of embracing either a gay or lesbian lifestyle is what is referred to as "coming out" (of the closet). Carmen De Monteflores and Stephen Schulz (1978, pp. 60-61) define this as the process through which gays and lesbians "recognize their sexual preferences and choose to integrate this knowledge into their personal and social lives," and add that this process is "marked by a series of milestone experiences, including awareness of same-sex attractions, first same-sex experience, coming out to friends, family, and coworkers, and coming out publicly." Coming out can be a painful process. It entails a decision to accept the role of a deviant in society and the possibility of being rejected by one's loved ones and friends. Youthful homosexuals are also faced with a lack of role models and uncertainty about how and where to contact like-minded persons. Sexual experimentation as a road to self-discovery has become increasingly blocked for young gays since the AIDS crisis.

"New gay" lesbians, however, tend to take a different route to a lesbian lifestyle. Lillian Faderman (1984) notes that these women discover and create their lesbianism within the context of feminism. They start with a critical evaluation of society and then consciously choose lesbianism as an alternative to heterosexual relationships, irrespective of their initial sexual feelings and desires.

Anthropological evidence points to the fact that the earlier-mentioned stage models may only apply in Western cultures, and that the development of either a gay or lesbian identity and lifestyle can differ considerably in cultures where other definitions of male and female gender roles exist. In any event, it seems obvious that one's homosexual feelings, desires, and fantasies lie partially outside the realm of free choice. On the other hand, one's decision to identify oneself as "gay" or "lesbian," to enter a homosexual subculture, or to initiate a stable homosexual relationship entails more of a voluntary decision. There are, of course, strong and sometimes highly divergent familial, peer, societal, and personal pressures that make the elements of decision and choice very complicated and, on occasion, very painful. Escaping inner agony and the complications involved with secrecy are not easy when one is then to be faced by general hostility, the loss of loved ones, and loneliness. The rewards of being considered a "normal" man or woman should not be underestimated.

NEGATIVE ASPECTS OF BEING HOMOSEXUAL

Many negative aspects associated with being lesbian or gay have been touched on in the preceding passages, including prejudice and discrimination in mainstream society; the lack of various rights, such as the access to one's children; the problems associated with being labelled deviant by others, status degradation and persecution; feelings of guilt, and the lack of self-acceptance, and self-esteem; relationship problems, especially with respect to exclusivity; and last, but not least, the intense fear, and threats to life and lifestyle brought about by AIDS.

The gay and lesbian subcultures play an important role in coping with the problematic aspects of being homosexual. For lesbians, the women's movement and second-wave feminism (which arose in the sixties) have provided a source of positive identity, a sense of community and solidarity that has helped overcome outside adversity. The ideological support that these movements have offered lesbians has helped them cope with their deviant status and facilitated coming out. Insights derived from feminism can be used to justify and legitimize the choice of another woman as a (sexual) partner. Not surprisingly, Peplau and her associates (1978) found that 80% of their sample of lesbians reported never feeling guilty about their sexual activities. The relatively recent integration of women into the workforce and their drive for equal rights and financial independence have also made it easier to afford leading a lesbian lifestyle without the pervasive fear of poverty.

Gays have had to face extreme sanctions for their behavior in the past. Whereas lesbians could expect financial disaster and shunning behavior, those who adopted a gay lifestyle were subjected to severe social ostracism, loss of employment (also leading to poverty), and official prosecution. At the individual level, this was reflected by a sense of guilt, shame, failure, and a loss of self-esteem (Schur, 1965). The necessity to conceal one's true feelings from others also had its psychological toll. However, the emergence of the gay subculture and gay communities throughout the western world has served to mitigate many of the distressing elements associated with gay life in the past by enhancing group cohesion and morale: by providing a sense of security, solidarity and belonging; offering access to other gays; creating a more positive self-identity; boosting of self-esteem; providing insight into the sources of social oppression; and by isolating gays from the hostile attitudes of the outside world.

In short, in the gay community, desires and behavior that constitute deviance in mainstream society are reevaluated and considered healthy and normal. Homosexual behavior is rewarded, and channels of expression are created. The other side of the coin is that gay communities tend to keep gays out of public view in the same way that ghettos keep poverty out of the average American's view, and many feel that if a true integration of lesbians and gays into the mainstream is to be the ultimate goal of the enduring struggle for emancipation and acceptance, then more is needed than a community to take refuge in. But not everyone is convinced that total integration is desirable. Some lesbians and gays, for instance, fear that the feeling of community and many of their unique cultural expressions and lifestyle patterns will then have to be

In my case, I was five years into my marriage before I really accepted that I was homosexual. I had known it very early and had gone to my minister in a small town in Oregon when I was 14 or 15 years old and told him I thought I was a homosexual. He was outraged at the notion and angrily told me I didn't conform to what a homosexual is like, wanting to wear a dress and makeup and all of that. He observed that I was a star student and a star athlete, and said I couldn't possibly be one of those vile people and it would be a disgrace to my family. I went away convinced that I was a heterosexual. When I went to college in Portland, a psychiatrist gave me a much more sophisticated version of the same kind of don't-give-me-this-nonsense treatment, and I ended up marrying and fathering three children. I was married for 11 years. About the middle of my marriage I began to realize that I had been living a lie, that I had been misled, and to use a rather graphic term, that I had been brainwashed. It's what a great many people in our society experience, both men and women, because they haven't been taught there are estimable people who are homosexuals.

Figure 4.2   There are multiple barriers to accepting a homosexual identity

surrendered. Nevertheless, without changes in society-at-large, homosexuals will always be stigmatized as deviant and consequently denied full participation in this society.

Another reason why the gay and lesbian communities are so vital is that gays and lesbians can expect less emotional support from their families than heterosexual couples. For many, disclosing one's homosexuality to parents and relatives is the last milestone on the way to assuming a positive homosexual identity. Because parents tend to have difficulty accepting their offsprings' homosexuality, their gay and lesbian children are more dependent upon friends for emotional support (Blumstein and Schwartz, 1983; Kurdek and Schmitt, 1987; McWhirter and Mattison, 1984).

The primary changes in the gay world during the past decades can be seen as an opening up, an awakening, a more relaxed attitude, the emergence of more expansive facilities, and a newly found sense of pride. The eighties, however, will probably go into the history books as the decade that has influenced the lifestyle of gays more than any other decade in this century. The reason is, of course, the disastrous impact of AIDS on the lives of many gay men. As this chapter is being written, some 15,000 homosexual men in the United States have died, and with no cure in sight, tens of thousands risk a similar fate. Although AIDS has affected other segments of the population and is now spreading among heterosexuals, the lives of gays have been hardest hit. As one newspaper comments: "Every aspect of their lives has been jarred by the crisis — their relationships, self-image, lifestyle, civil rights, sexuality" (*Los Angeles Times,* November 13, 1985).

The psychological problems associated with being diagnosed as having AIDS are manifold. Stephen Morin and his associates (1984, p. 1288) summarize these as follows:

> The usual psychological reactions that accompany the diagnosis include fear of death and dying, guilt, fear of exposure of life-style, fear of contagion, loss of self-esteem, fear of loss of physical attractiveness, fears of decreased social support and increased dependency, isolation and stigmatization, loss of occupational and financial status, concerns and confusion over options for medical treatment, and the overriding sense of gloom and helplessness associated with a degenerative illness.

It is not difficult to imagine the extreme anxiety and distress among many gays that they might have contracted AIDS at some time in the past. The long incubation period can prolong fears for several years. The gay community and various self-help organizations, such as Shanti in San Francisco, serve a very important role in helping gays who are fearful of contracting AIDS, who have scored sero-positive on tests, or who have already contracted the disease, to cope with their concerns, feelings, pains, and suffering. Fortunately, because the major gay communities were already somewhat organized, it has been easier to mobilize various resources and develop strategies to alleviate some of the confusion and suffering that would otherwise have been rampant. In the future it will be especially the homosexual communities that will help homosexuals come to grips with the obstacles put in their path to a gratifying life.

The major effect of the AIDS crisis with respect to the male homosexual's way of life has been the radical inhibition of the promiscuous lifestyle that was characteristic of many gays, and consequently the decline of those elements in the subculture that catered to the sexual needs of these men. The number of casual sexual contacts has dropped significantly and "safe sex" has become the new motto. When this type of sex is practiced, there is no oral sex with semen exchange and no anal sex without condoms (Richardson, 1986). Some men are even practicing celibacy. The number of gays in San Francisco that now claim to be either monogamous, celibate, or only perform "unsafe" sex with their steady partner has gradually risen from 69% to 81%. Consequently, venereal disease, highly prevalent among gays in the past, dropped 80% in this group between 1981 and 1985 in New York (*Los Angeles Times,* November 13, 1985). Those who still have multiple anonymous and "unsafe" sexual encounters may afterwards suffer from panic attacks, fear, and/or guilt. One sex therapist was quoted as follows: "I used to encourage gay clients to go out to a bar and pick up people, to try out, explore, and experiment with lots of different aspects of their sexuality. . . . Now with AIDS, I'm needing to do the opposite" (Morin et al., 1984). To fulfill the gay's sexual needs in a safer manner, some novel activities have emerged. These include telephone sex for erotic conversations, classes in nonorgasmic sex, X-rated video movies, and masturbation and massage parties. Another development is that intimacy has become a more salient goal than it was before.

The AIDS epidemic has struck at the very heart of the gay subculture: 64% of all cases are presently found in the four earlier mentioned cities of San Francisco, New York, Los Angeles, and Miami (Batchelor, 1984). Many bathhouses have been closed during the past few years. Some of these have been closed down by the authorities (in New York, for instance), while others have gone out of business for lack of customers or because of the fear of spreading the disease. There are indications, however, that despite the general panic, fear, and pain that AIDS has inflicted on the gay communities throughout the nation, these communities have become more cohesive than they used to be. Under the pressure of the crisis at hand, many previously secretive gays are also acknowledging their homosexuality and joining the gay community.

In closing, we might add that the AIDS crisis has had little or no effect on the nature of lesbian relationships, since those involved in such relationships have almost no chance of contracting AIDS, no matter how promiscuous they are with other women.

REVIEW QUESTIONS

1) What functions does the homosexual subculture fulfill for homosexuals?
2) What effect has the AIDS crisis had on the homosexual community? How about its effect on public attitudes towards homosexuals?
3) How do homosexual relationships differ from heterosexual relationships? What makes homosexual relationships so unstable?

SUGGESTED PROJECTS

1) Ask two people you know why they think people become homosexual. Which of the models discussed in this chapter do their responses reflect?
2) Step a) Make a list of all the potential keywords you think you might find in a newspaper index that will offer information on homosexuality.

Step b) Using the list of keywords you've made, go to the library and look through one or several indexes of the *New York Times* or a different newspaper for articles pertaining to homosexuality.

Step c) What keywords do the selected newspapers use?

Step d) How many articles can you find on homosexuality?

Step e) Read the five most recent articles.

Step f) Make a summary of the newspaper coverage you've read.

3) Fig. 4.1 lists the maximum jail sentences for sodomy in U.S. states. Determine what the maximum jail sentence was for your state in 1986. Did this apply to homosexual sodomy only? (If you live in Canada or elsewhere, skip this question and fill in "province" or "nation" where we refer to "state" in the remainder of this assignment.) Next, go to the library and try to find out what changes have taken place in your state between 1945 and the present.

5

Extramarital Relationships

DEFINING EXTRAMARITAL RELATIONSHIPS

UNLIKE THE OTHER CHAPTERS in this book, the present chapter deals with married people. It does, however, concern a specific subgroup, namely those who get involved in sexual relationships outside of their marriage. It can be stated without exaggeration that an extramarital relationship is usually seen as a violation of one of the basic assumptions of marriage, namely that it should be sexually exclusive. Nevertheless, there are a substantial number of people who, for various reasons and under a wide variety of circumstances, become involved in such relationships. There are divergent patterns of extramarital relationships, such as married individuals who conduct secretive affairs, couples involved in "mate swapping," and sexually "open" marriages. All these patterns are referred to here as "sexually nonexclusive" marriages, and the term "extramarital relationship" is used to describe all sexual involvements outside of marriage. It must be noted that the word "extramarital" literally means "outside of marriage." Accordingly, all kinds of relationships with someone other than the spouse, including nonsexual ones, constitute, strictly speaking, extramarital relationships. However, the term extramarital is usually restricted to sexual relationships, and this general usage is followed here.

"Adultery," "infidelity," and "unfaithfulness" are some of the words often used in our language to designate extramarital relationships, reflecting the common notion that sexual involvements of married people with others constitute a betrayal of the spouse. However, such betrayal is not necessarily the case. A minority of extramarital affairs do occur with the knowledge and approval of the spouse, and some authors have suggested reserving the term "comarital" for such relationships, and to restrict the word extramarital only to relationships that are more or less competitive with marital relationships (Roy and Roy, 1973). Nevertheless, we prefer to view the term extramarital relationship as a merely descriptive term that may refer to such diverse meanings and patterns as cheating, unfaithfulness, infidelity, adultery, swinging, and sexually open marriages. Although sexual contacts with prostitutes can, in a theoretical sense, also be seen as extramarital relationships, they will not be discussed in this chapter.

SOCIETAL CONTEXT

Incidence in Society

Extramarital affairs have surfaced wherever marriages have existed. In ancient Rome, for instance, many wealthy women turned to adultery as a way of expressing their individuality. In medieval England, adultery between servants and masters was widespread, partially due to the fact that separate sleeping arrangements were unknown, and that the bedrooms (if they existed) were overcrowded. Among the nobility in Europe of the past, where arranged marriages were common, men often expressed their longings for sex, love, and romance in relationships with mistresses. According to the English historian Lawrence Stone (1977), seventeenth-century England under Charles II saw a dramatic upsurge in extramarital liaisons among members of the court aristocracy, spreading slowly down to agricultural society. Sexual promiscuity became a hallmark of fashion at court and in high political circles, and the crude word "adultery" became replaced by the more attractive word "gallantry." Wives of all social levels seem to have been rather indifferent to the adulterous behavior of their husbands, and did not mind the fact that this behavior was sometimes publicly visible. Similar patterns prevailed in France during the same period, where one of the most famous mistresses in history, Madame de Pompadour, exerted considerable political power because King Louis XV had no taste for government. Other types of extramarital involvements have been noted in Europe's past. For example, in eighteenth-century France there even appear to have been incidents of mate swapping among actors and actresses (Murstein, 1974).

There is very little reliable data on the incidence of extramarital relationships in contemporary American society. To obtain such data, one needs a representative sample, as well as a methodology that insures honest answers. Few studies in this area have met both requirements. For example, in the well-known Kinsey studies, it was estimated that about 40% of the males and 26% of the females had experienced extramarital coitus by age forty. However, Kinsey did not have random or representative samples, and it seems likely that his estimates were too high, especially when taking into account the early date at which the data were gathered. Similar restrictions apply to the study by Philip Blumstein and Pepper Schwartz (1983) who found that after ten years or more together, 30% of the married men and 22% of the married women had had at least one extramarital affair. After reviewing twelve surveys of extramarital behavior, Anthony Thompson (1983) concluded the probability that at least one partner in a marriage will have an extramarital relationship lies somewhere between 40% and 76%. Since sexually liberal subjects are probably overrepresented in most samples, the latter figure may be too high. But even if the lowest estimate is correct, it would mean that nearly half of all American marriages are in one way or another affected by extramarital involvements. It must be emphasized, however, that in many of these cases an extramarital affair happens only once or twice in the lifetime of the individual involved, especially among women (Pietropinto and Simenauer, 1977; Blumstein and Schwartz, 1983).

Attitudes in Society

While in many cases extramarital relationships were readily accepted in the past by the general populace, extramarital sex has traditionally been *officially* condemned in Western society quite strongly. The Roman Catholic and Protestant religions disapproved of this behavior unequivocally, although it took centuries before the church managed to take control of marriage law in which adultery was forbidden. In the traditional Catholic view, even a second marriage was considered adultery if the spouse was still alive. Protestantism was hardly more tolerant. One of its founders, Calvin, "hated adultery with a deadly passion" (Cole, 1969). Both Calvin and Luther argued that it should be a capital crime. While in Europe legal punishment of adulterers was mostly rather lenient, adulterers in the early New England colonies were sometimes, indeed, put to death. Even today, extramarital sex is a crime in many American states, although these laws are seldom enforced.

At present, a large majority (over 75%) of the American adult population still unequivocally disapproves of extramarital sex (Glenn and Weaver, 1979), while in Western European countries extramarital sex is more often accepted. For instance, Harold Christensen (1973) compared the attitudes of students at different American universities with student attitudes in other countries. One of the results of his study was that, with the exception of a black American university, the percentage of people voicing unqualified disapproval of extramarital coitus was much higher in all of the American universities sampled than in the Swedish, Danish, and Belgian universities. Relatively tolerant attitudes toward this behavior are also found in the Netherlands. Opinions in the Netherlands about extramarital sex have changed considerably since the 1960s. In 1965, 78% of the adult population considered this behavior to be wrong in all cases. This figure decreased to about 50% in 1975, and to 45% in 1981, a figure much lower than in the United States. Men are much more tolerant than women in this respect: 37% versus 54% consider extramarital sex wrong in all cases (Schelvis, 1983).

Although many societies tend to be more tolerant than the United States, it is remarkable that no society gives its members complete freedom to engage in extramarital sex. Anthropological studies show that even in societies that approve of extramarital relationships, these relationships are specified and restricted in one way or another. For example, in some societies extramarital sex is only allowed with siblings-in-law, while in other instances men are granted sexual access to the wife of other men on special occasions, such as when they are a guest (Ford and Beach, 1952). Also, disapproval of extramarital relationships in Western societies is dependent upon the nature of the extramarital involvement. A study in Australia by Anthony Thompson (1984) shows that different types of extramarital involvement are viewed differently, dependent upon the extent of emotional and sexual involvement. Relationships that were emotional and sexual were judged as more wrong than purely sexual relationships, while purely sexual relationships were rated as more wrong than purely emotional involvements.

Despite the general disapproval of sex outside of marriage, in most cultures, as well as in Western culture in the past, a double standard has been quite common, making adultery engaged in by men much easier to forgive than adultery by women, and favoring strong sanctions against female adultery. In England of the past, for instance, adultery was a male prerogative, while the sexual behavior of women before and outside of marriage was constrained in every possible way, preventing any doubts about the legitimacy of the offspring (Stone, 1977). Such attitudes have been found all over the world. Traditional Greek norms, for example, gave a husband the right to kill his wife as a matter of "honor" if she engaged in extramarital sex. Unfaithfulness of the husband was not considered to be a crime; it was seen as a normal consequence of the polygamous nature of men (Safilios-Rothschild, 1969). Until quite recently in France, the *crime passionel* was acceptable primarily for men, not for women; in Belgium only the wife's infidelity constituted legal grounds for divorce. In contemporary North

When Jon Slohoda filed for divorce and moved in with a female co-worker, he never expected his employer to fire him for adultery.

Slohoda, 29, was a manager at the UPS center in Bound Brook, N.J., for 10 years before he was fired in November 1981. He contends he was dismissed unfairly because he was living with a female co-worker while separated from his wife. UPS did not fire single employees who cohabitate, he said.

UPS lawyers, arguing that management should be allowed to fire workers for adultery, said there is a distinction between sex involving two single adults and adultery involving at least one married person.

Slohoda's lawyer Nancy Smith said that her client had filed for divorce before moving in with the UPS employee, Patricia Arnette, and that they later were married. Arnette, a supervisor, was unmarried and was not fired. The case "could have very broad implications," said Smith. "Are they going to set up surveillance teams in people's bedrooms to see who they are sleeping with? The idea of having so-called moral standards being applied to employees invades their right to privacy."

Although the appeals panel ruled on a narrow element of case — that using different standards for married and single employees violated discrimination laws — the court went further and said it remains to be proven whether Slohoda's right of privacy might have been violated.

Figure 5.1   Adultery is still subjected to social disapproval

Source: San Francisco Chronicle, February 9, 1984.

America, where a single standard of sexual behavior has become widely accepted, residues of the double standard may still surface at times. Indeed, a recent survey showed that extramarital sex engaged in by women was condemned by (slightly) more people than similar behavior engaged in by men (McClosky and Brill, 1983).

VARIETIES OF EXTRAMARITAL BEHAVIOR PATTERNS

There is a tremendous diversity of extramarital behaviors. Sexual relationships outside of marriage can be surrounded by a variety of values, norms, and ideologies. They can arise from various motivations, can take place in divergent social contexts and places, and can vary considerably in duration and depth of involvement. Illustrative is the classical study by John Cuber (1969) that showed the existence of three distinct types of marriages with extramarital relationships. First, such relationships may compensate for a defective marriage that is continued primarily because of social pressure. In such cases, the extramarital relationship may often resemble a marital relationship, including the norm of sexual exclusivity. A second type of marriage includes couples that, because of their professional obligations for example, are often separated, and have agreed upon casual affairs. For these couples, a sexually exclusive marriage may also be the preferred state, despite their behavior. This is, however, not at all the case for the third type of couples, what Cuber calls the "true Bohemians," who do not recognize monogamy and fully sanction extramarital relationships. Despite the significance of Cuber's work, his typology is not complete or exhaustive. For example, there are those married individuals who occasionally have more or less secret extramarital affairs, mainly for the sake of variety or because the circumstances promote it, but who love their spouse and have no intention whatsoever of getting a divorce. In this pattern, attitudes toward extramarital sex will tend to be ambivalent, and there is usually no open discussion of the issue. The spouse is either unaware of such involvements, or suspects it but tolerates it as long as it does not infringe upon the marriage. There can also be a tacit understanding that both spouses can have their share of extramarital relationships as long as it is handled discreetly.

Quite different is the "sexually open marriage" (Knapp and Whitehurst, 1977; Buunk, 1980b; Watson, 1981), a type of nonexclusive union that is closely related to the third type mentioned by Cuber (1969). The concept of the open marriage gained wide visibility and notoriety through a book by Nena and George O'Neill (1972). As indicated in Chapter 1, they described open marriage as a lifestyle that emphasizes living in the "here-and-now," with realistic expectations, equality and role flexibility, respect for personal privacy, autonomy and independence, combined with trust, and honest and open communication. Instead of advocating extramarital sex, as has often mistakenly been assumed, the O'Neills had a neutral attitude toward such behavior, and did not view involvement in extramarital relationships as a typical aspect of open marriages. Nevertheless, they considered it possible for some couples to integrate such relationships into an open marriage. From our perspective, sexually open marriages are all those marriages in which both spouses have a positive attitude toward extramarital relationships and give each other the freedom to pursue such relationships under certain conditions, and where both spouses actually do have such relationships. These relationships can vary from "one-night stands" to long-lasting affairs.

"Swinging" is a nonexclusive pattern that is generally viewed as quite distinct from sexually open marriages, although in this arrangement, both spouses also approve of, and actually do have, extramarital relationships. However, in this case these relationships are restricted to contexts in which both engage in such behavior at the same time and usually in the same place. In swinging, the pursuit of extramarital relationships is primarily by means of some organized or institutionalized pattern; they are usually not spontaneous occurrences (Walshok, 1971). Swinging couples meet each other through personal reference, public or private "swinging" clubs, or through advertisements in specialized magazines or in newspapers. A distinction is made between open and closed swinging, depending on whether sexual activities take place in the same room or in separate rooms. In closed swinging, sexual encounters can be restricted to two couples, or can take place at parties attended by many couples. In open swinging, several persons can engage in genital contact at the same time. In such situations, homosexuality is rare for males, yet common for females. Sometimes, games such as stripping are used as an "ice-breaker." Characteristic of swinging is that it is often highly regulated. It is only engaged in as a couple, both spouses have to approve, and independently conducted affairs as well as emotional involvement are to be avoided (Denfeld and Gordon, 1970). There are many swingers, however, who look for, and develop intimate friendships with other couples (Gilmartin, 1974). This is probably especially true at present, due to the fear of contracting AIDS.

There is also a clear tendency in sexually open marriages to regulate extramarital behavior as a way of preventing potential damage to the marriage relationship. In their study of American couples, Blumstein and Schwartz (1983) emphasize that all successful open relationships have built-in rules, whether or not the couple realizes it. A wide range of different patterns of ground rules have been reported, which all seem to fall somewhere between the extremes of secret affairs on the one hand, and "swinging" on the other. The following patterns have been identified by Dutch social psychologist Bram Buunk (1980b).

1) Marriage primacy. This includes all the ground rules which in one way or another uphold honesty and loyalty toward the spouse as a central value. For example, a very large majority in Buunk's (1980b) sample attached great importance to this. Respondents stressed that extramarital relationships were only permissible provided that the participants follow a policy of absolute honesty, always put the marriage relationship first, show respect for the feelings of all involved, and devote a sufficient amount of time and energy to the partner. Other studies have found comparable ground rules such as the rule that one should avoid potential partners who are looking for a new primary relationship, and that honesty in giving information to extramarital partners is of paramount importance (Watson, 1981).

2) *Restricted intensity.* In this pattern, the marital relationship is protected by restricting the intimacy and degree of involvement in the extramarital affairs. In Buunk's (1980b) study, more than one-third of the respondents felt that the extramarital contacts should not become too intense, while a small group even wished to limit themselves and their partners to brief contacts only. In addition, about one-third subscribed to the rule that an extramarital relationship should be terminated at the request of the spouse. Those insisting upon such rules place strong limitations upon themselves and their spouses with respect to the spontaneous development of extramarital relationships. Apparently, the preservation of the central importance of the marriage outweighs any feelings of attraction that may exist outside it, no matter how strong.

3) *Visibility.* A definite tendency toward protecting the marital relationship by restricting the behavior options with regard to extramarital relationships can also be seen in this pattern. It includes different rules aimed at keeping the spouse as knowledgeable as possible of one's involvements. An important ground rule found by Mary Ann Watson (1981), for instance, was that appropriate and inappropriate partners were agreed upon by the couple. While this implied the exclusion of close personal friends and business associates for most subjects in Watson's sample, in Buunk's study (1980b) the opposite was found; many subjects emphasized the restriction of extramarital relationships to people known to the other spouse. In addition, some found the simultaneous occurrence of more than one extramarital relationship unacceptable, while other respondents considered prior consultation with their spouse an absolute requirement.

4) *Invisibility.* While the foregoing patterns all had something in common with "swinging," this pattern is closer to secret affairs. These arrangements often include ground rules that allow both spouses a certain amount of freedom to develop extramarital relationships as long as the nonparticipating partner is not too aware of what is taking place. This pattern was only found in a small subgroup of Buunk's (1980b) sample, but may well be quite prevalent in sexually nonexclusive marriages.

Despite the attention given here to extramarital relationships that occur with the knowledge and approval of the spouse, such behaviors seem to constitute only a minority of all extramarital involvements. In their study of American couples, Blumstein and Schwartz (1983) found that married couples were more secretive about sex outside the relationship than gay, lesbian, and cohabiting couples. Given the likely overrepresentation of sexual liberals in Morton Hunt's (1974) study conducted on behalf of *Playboy* magazine, it is striking that most (about four-fifths) of the extramarital relationships occurred without the knowledge of the spouse. These findings suggest that sexually open marriages are a rather rare phenomenon. This can also be concluded from the small percentage of people in American society who express an unequivocally positive attitude towards extramarital relationships. In 1977, only 3% to 4% of the American population considered extramarital sex not at all wrong (Glenn and Weaver, 1979). This seems to indicate the upper limit of the percentage of people who are involved in sexually open marriages. There is a similar lack of reliable data concerning the incidence of swinging. Nevertheless, reviewing the various incidence estimates, Bernard Murstein (1978) suggests that perhaps, at most, about 250,000 couples are regular swingers, although many more couples have tried swinging. Recently, however, because of the fear of AIDS, interest in swinging seems to have declined considerably.

CHARACTERISTICS OF THOSE INCLINED TOWARD EXTRAMARITAL INVOLVEMENT

Many studies have shown that extramarital sex is accepted more easily, and is also more prevalent among persons with certain demographic, attitudinal, and behavioral characteristics (Reiss, 1981). It must be emphasized, however, that there are some methodological problems inherent in research on extramarital relationships. First, many survey studies have only assessed the *attitudes* toward sex outside marriage, which are known to be poor indicators of actual extramarital sexual behavior. Second, given the taboo nature of the subject, it is difficult to get valid data on behavior in survey research. Extramarital behavior may be more taboo for some (women, religious individuals) than for others. A consequence of this could be that a higher incidence of extramarital sex found in certain categories primarily reflects a higher willingness to *report* this behavior, and not necessarily a higher prevalence of extramarital sex. Third, studies examining individuals involved in specific extramarital behaviors have often employed samples of convenience that may not be representative of all individuals involved in such behaviors.

Despite these qualifications, the following can, though with some caution, be said about the variables related to extramarital behaviors and attitudes:

1) Gender. Many studies have found that, generally speaking, males have a more positive attitude towards extramarital sex, particularly towards the more casual variants of it. Men also fantasize more about sexual involvement outside of their marriage and are more inclined to engage in such behavior when the opportunity presents itself. For instance, in a recent Australian study, Thompson (1984) found that women were more disapproving of sexual relationships outside marriage, and were less likely than men to pursue such relationships. As far as actual behavior is concerned, however, several studies have found that women in the younger age groups, and especially liberated women, are presently catching up with the men (Hunt, 1974; Buunk, 1980a). However, recent research shows that still more men than women are involved in extramarital affairs, and that among those with extramarital experience, men are more likely than women to have had extramarital intercourse without emotional involvement (Pepper and Schwartz, 1983; Glass and Wright, 1985).

2) Age. A recurrent finding is that older people tend to be less permissive towards extramarital sex. Those who have been extramaritally involved have been so later in their marriage than younger people, probably because they had to overcome more moral barriers (Hunt, 1974). It is doubtful, however, whether aging makes people more reluctant to engage in extramarital sex. Studies of sexually open marriages suggest, for example, that such arrangements are only started by couples when they have been married for more than five to ten years (Ramey, 1975). As we will discuss later, this is not true of many individuals who get divorced after having been involved in extramarital affairs.

3) Education, social class and urban background. Many studies have shown that extramarital sex is *not* consistently more prevalent at certain social levels. However, higher educated individuals from the upper middle classes have a more favorable attitude toward extramarital sex (Reiss, 1980; Weis and Jurich, 1985), and are more inclined to become involved in such behaviors, particularly in experimental varieties, such as sexually open marriages. The same is true for swinging, although some older studies found that swingers had a somewhat lower educational and professional level than those involved in other forms of "consensual adultery"(Bartell, 1971). Furthermore, it must be noted that in general, a more positive attitude toward extramarital sex is found in urban areas than in rural areas (Weiss and Jurich, 1985).

4) Religion. As is true for other more or less deviant sexual behavior, religious individuals tend to disapprove relatively strongly of extramarital sex, and various extramarital behaviors are much more prevalent among persons who do not consider themselves to be religious. This holds true whether one measures frequency of church attendance or religious beliefs. For example, Brian Gilmartin (1974, pp. 302-303) found that nearly two-thirds of his sample of swingers, as compared to one-quarter of a control group, agreed with the statement "religion is one of the greatest sources of hate, intolerance and oppression that the world has ever known."

5) Political views. In general, positive attitudes toward extramarital sex, as well as actual extramarital involvements, are more prevalent among the politically liberal (Singh et al., 1976). Minako Maykovich (1976) found that American women with extramarital sex experience have more positive attitudes toward the women's liberation movement, and toward legalized prostitution. Although such liberal attitudes are also common among couples with sexually open marriages, less consensus exists with respect to the question of whether swingers are relatively liberal or conservative. For example, Gilbert Bartell (1971) indicated that this sample was generally ethnocentric and had conservative political views, while Brian Gilmartin (1974) found his sample of swingers to be quite liberal on issues varying from sex education to civil rights. A solution to this contradiction was offered by Richard Jenks (1985a), who showed that swingers were (compared to a control group) relatively liberal on issues related to their own sexual behavior (such as abortion, pornography, and divorce), but more conservative on issues completely unrelated to their sexual lifestyle. For example, swingers were more in favor of capital punishment, wanted to spend less on welfare, were less supportive of controlling business and industry, and had a less positive attitude towards the Equal Rights Amendment.

6) Attitude towards sexuality. The inclination to engage in extramarital sex is clearly related to a positive attitude toward other sexual behaviors such as premarital sex and sexual experimentation within marriage. Premarital sexual permissiveness is closely related to a positive attitude towards extramarital sex (Weis and Jurich, 1985). Furthermore, persons who had been involved in extramarital sex report more premarital partners and more diverse sexual activities. Thus, Robert Bell and his colleagues (1975) found that women who had masturbated during their marriage, women who liked oral sex, and women who had been exposed to pornography, had more often been involved in extramarital coitus.

7) Marital dissatisfaction. Dissatisfaction with the quality of marriage in general, and with the sexual relationship in particular, is associated with a positive attitude toward extramarital sex, as well as with fantasizing about it, and with actually engaging in such behavior. Among men, dissatisfaction in the beginning of marriage seems to lead to extramarital sex, while among women this is particularly the case in later stages (Glass and Wright, 1977). Furthermore, extramarital sex is more closely related to sexual deprivation in marriage for men than for women. At the same time, for women marital dissatisfaction is more strongly linked to emotional involvement in extramarital affairs (Glass and Wright, 1985). In sexually open marriages, however, motives other than marital dissatisfaction seem to prevail, and such marriages have been found to be as happy as comparable monogamous marriages (Rubin, 1983). In two independent studies it was found that extramarital relationships that occur with the approval of the spouse reflect a better marital relationship than those which are not accepted by the spouse (Buunk, 1980a; Gilmartin, 1974).

8) Personality and mental health. Some therapists maintain that involvement in extramarital affairs often stems from psychological problems, such as the seeking of narcissistic joy, a low frustration tolerance, the insatiable thirst for confirmation of manhood, or escapism (see also Pietropinto and Simenauer, 1977). These are certainly undue generalizations, since the findings on this issue are rather complex and contradictory. Most studies do not show those involved in extramarital relationships to be personally less adequate (Murstein et al., 1985). Nevertheless, there is *some* evidence that points to mental health problems among a group of individuals who engage in extramarital sex. First, extramarital relationships have in some studies been found to be more prevalent among men who feel alienated from life (Whitehurst, 1969). Second, although a study by Mary Ann Watson (1981) showed that participants in sexually open marriages were self-assured, flexible, independent, and tolerant, the same study found that no less than 74% of this sample had been in marital therapy with their spouse. Third, swingers in Gilmartin's (1974) study had been in psychotherapy much more often than a control group of nonswingers, and had more often experienced an unhappy adolescence and distant insensitive parental attitudes, although they scored lower in anomie and alcohol intake. Finally, in another study of swingers, Jane Duckworth and Eugene Levitt (1985), using one of the most widely accepted personality tests, the MMPI, concluded that no less than half of the sample were emotionally disturbed and that nearly a quarter of the sample might be considered to be emotionally disturbed enough to require professional intervention. Although this last study has been rightfully criticized by Constantine (1985), it can be stated on the basis of all the foregoing studies that probably a significant minority of people involved in extramarital relationships, particularly among swingers, experience some psychological problems. It is interesting to note that while many proponents of open arrangements base themselves in humanistic psychology, the founder of this school of thought, Abraham Maslow (1970), stated that the prototypes of excellent mental health, the self-actualizers, were relatively more monogamous than the average individual, and less apt to have affairs.

GETTING INVOLVED: PROCESSES AND MOTIVATIONS

Divergent factors may lead to involvement in extramarital relationships. When such relationships stem from a certain philosophy, as is the case with most sexually open marriages, or when they take place in organized settings, as is true for most swinging activities, then extramarital sexual involvement may be a deliberate, premeditated action. In other instances, an extramarital affair may happen unexpectedly when the opportunity presents itself, or when the person is psychologically ripe for an extramarital encounter. Becoming involved in extramarital relationships often implies a decision process in which the costs and benefits are identified, and are compared with the expected values of alternative decisions. Ralph Meyering and Elizabeth Epling-McWerther (1986) studied such decision processes and found that men were more affected by the perceived payoffs, including variation; and women more by the costs, including the probability of strong guilt feelings and the marriage being negatively affected. Whatever the perceived costs and benefits may be, in most cases an extramarital relationship is the result of a process in which people gradually move toward actually becoming involved. According to Lynn Atwater (1979), the feasibility of engaging in extramarital sex is facilitated by such factors as receiving invitations from members of the opposite sex, knowing someone who has already experienced an extramarital relationship, discussing the matter with others, as well as thinking about getting involved. The importance of such factors was illuminated by Buunk (1980a), who showed that actual involvement in extramarital sex

was strongly related to approval of this behavior by friends and acquaintances, the proportion of one's reference group that had engaged
in this behavior, and the number of times a third person had clearly
indicated a desire to have sexual contact within the preceding year.

It is difficult to assess objectively what factors make people actually
become involved in extramarital relationships. The reasons they themselves tend to offer cannot always be considered convincing evidence.
As sociologist Lynn Atwater (1979) has pointed out, people may often
give two different types of explanations for their extramarital behavior:
justifications and *excuses*. Justifications are aimed at keeping one's
self-image intact by accepting the responsibility for one's behavior, but
denying that there is anything wrong with it. Atwater found that women
gave justifications more frequently than excuses and that the theme of
self-fulfillment was the pervasive one of all the justifications. Excuses,
the category of explanations in which people deny responsibility for
their actions but accept the negative value of their acts, were offered in
about one-quarter of the cases, and comprised a pattern of "it just
happened" statements. Other research shows that individuals who have
affairs but who maintain an ideology of exclusivity are inclined to
excuse their affairs by pointing to a lack of satisfaction in their own
marriage (Buunk, 1987a). In general, people who make excuses tend to
favor monogamous marriage. They see monogamy as the ideal situation, but dissatisfactions in their own marriage bring them to rationalize
and participate in extramarital relationships (Gerstel, 1979). Persons in
such a situation may stay married for a variety of reasons, such as social
pressure, children, economic factors, and a certain attachment to the
spouse.

Of course, not all the reasons that are offered for getting involved in
extramarital relationships should be considered excuses or justifications. It will become clear, however, that the foregoing analysis is quite
relevant when dealing with the motivations mentioned by individuals
who have had extramarital affairs. Major motivations include the following:

1) Opportunity. External circumstances, such as opportunities due to
temporary separation, are often considered to be very important in
stimulating involvement in extramarital affairs. In one study, it was
mentioned by no less than 81% of those involved in extramarital affairs
(Buunk, 1984). Also, in a study of commuter marriages (couples who
lived apart for professional reasons at least three days a week), individuals who embraced an ideal of monogamy tended to excuse
their extramarital involvement by pointing to external circumstances

(Gerstel, 1979). However, in the same study it was shown that 60% of the commuters never, either before or while commuting, engaged in extramarital affairs. Most individuals who had started affairs after commuting had engaged in such behavior before. Even more striking evidence that physical separation does not in itself cause affairs comes from the fact that more people had affairs while they shared a single residence with their spouses than after they set up two separate households.

2) Reciprocity. There are couples who do not view sexual exclusivity as an ethical issue, but who refrain from extramarital relationships for reasons of reciprocity: "you don't, so I won't." Or, vice versa, other couples have a personal code of exchange that implies: since "you do, so will I" (Gerstel, 1979, p. 170); and some engage in extramarital sex out of revenge for the partner doing the same. Still other couples seem to turn things around once more and say: "I do, so you can too." In one study, high correlations were found between one's own inclination to become involved in extramarital relationships and the readiness to tolerate such behavior in the spouse (Buunk, 1982b). Apparently, some people justify their own involvement in extramarital affairs by stating they would accept similar behavior of their partner.

3) Higher order beliefs. According to Jacqueline Knapp and Robert Whitehurst (1979, p. 149), for many Americans involvement in sexually open marriage is part of what they see as the sacred obligation to live a full life — a sophisticated type of justification. Many respondents preferred sexually open marriages because they enabled them to live out their personal philosophies or beliefs. "As active seekers of utopian ideals . . . they appeared intellectually committed to sexual openness." This type of openness is motivated by values such as autonomy, independence, and freedom.

4) Novelty, variety, and excitement. Another type of motivation mentioned by people in many different types of extramarital involvements is a desire for novelty, variety, and excitement. In his pioneering book on extramarital relationships, Gerhard Neubeck (1969) suggested that, due to overexposure to the partner, a certain satiation occurs in many marriages, and that an extramarital partner often has the attractiveness of novelty. Jim Ramey (1975) found that exploring new aspects of one's personality, sexual exploration, and new experiences were important motives among those involved in sexually open marriage. Knapp and Whitehurst (1977) noted that such people sought variety, complexity, romance, courtship, and even problems to keep things lively. It is quite likely that similar motives also play a role for those involved in secretive extramarital affairs. Even more so, the secret aspect of it can add to the excitement. Furthermore, according to Atwater (1979), one basic script for extramarital sex is motivated by the desire for curiosity, new experience, and personal growth. Particularly men seem to attribute their extramarital liaisons to a need for sexual variety. Laurel Richardson (1985) suggests that, by defining their extramarital relationships as primarily sexual even if they are not, men have at their disposal a culturally legimated rationalization for extramarital involvements.

The search for variety and novelty seems to be the main motivation for swingers. According to Betty Fang (1976), the common motives to swing are boredom and restlessness; a need for new experiences; and motives directly related to problems in the marital relationship, such as looking for a means to patch up a failing marriage, and a desire for more sex than the partner is willing to offer.

5) *Dissatisfaction in marriage.* Meyering and Epling-McWerther (1986) reported that men used marital problems more often as a justification for extramarital sex than women. However, in the study by Atwater (1979) it was found that about half of the women who had been involved in extramarital relationships mentioned an unsatisfactory marriage as part of their motivation. Not all subjects in these studies had sexually open marriages, and one may wonder to what degree sexual non-exclusivity in such marriages is primarily motivated by dissatisfaction with the marital relationship. There are indications that for a number of individuals this is definitely the case, and that adherence to a philosophy of a sexually open marriage in such cases is, consciously or unconsciously, the first step towards ending the marriage (Watson, 1981). In any case, more than 40% of the subjects in a study by Buunk (1984) of sexually open marriages mentioned marital deprivation as a motivation. The issue is quite complex, however, since many participants in sexually open marriages embrace, as part of their philosophy, the belief that two people can never hope to satisfy all of each other's needs for happiness. Therefore, outside relationships are defined as necessary to relieve pressure within the marriage and provide a broader base for need-fulfillment and well-being (Knapp and Whitehurst, 1977).

6) *Love and friendship.* In general, love and friendship loom as important motivations for engaging in extramarital relationships.

Buunk (1980a) found that many married people (no less than 30%) said that they had been in love with someone other than their spouse during the year preceding the interview, and that this was the case for the majority of those who had had extramarital sex during that period. On the other hand, Atwater (1979) reports that only a minority of the women she interviewed stated they were in love with their extramarital partner. More often, the extramarital sex was part of a friendship, and it is indeed not uncommon that extramarital sex develops in the context of friendships with the opposite sex. Couples with sexually open marriages as well as swinging couples often build friendship networks of like-minded couples and singles, in which sexual relationships may take place. It must be noted, however, that the concept of friendship can have divergent meanings, and that this can lead to inequality in extramarital relationships. In her study *The Other Women,* Laurel Richardson (1985) emphasized that relationships between single women involved with married men are frequently defined as friendships. However, because friendship means different things to men and women, men often have an advantage over women in extramarital relationships. Not only do women define friendship as more intimate and involving, but they also expect themselves, as friends, to be agreeable, sympathetic, and forgiving. Men consider friendship more as buddyship. Because of such differences, the women in these relationships become more vulnerable than the men.

STAYING INVOLVED: POSITIVE AND NEGATIVE ASPECTS

Positive Aspects

People involved in extramarital relationships often find themselves in a situation where strong problems generated by their extramarital relationships conflict with the strong attraction to the extramarital partner (or to extramarital involvements in general). Indeed, such relationships often have a very high reward potential. In general, people report that extramarital relationships themselves are experienced quite positively. In a study conducted by Buunk (1980b), nearly all subjects emphasized the quality of the communication with the outside partner, and a large majority reported that new aspects of their personality emerged in this relationship. Half of the respondents indicated that the bond with the extramarital partner gradually became stronger. No less than three-fourths judged the sexual aspect of their extramarital relationship to be better than with their spouse in several respects. In

Atwater's (1982) study, about 60% of the women enjoyed sex more with their extramarital partner than with their husband. Many reported a sense of learning, self-recognition, and self-discovery as a consequence of the extramarital sexual experience. Swingers report similar positive sexual experiences, including shedding of sexual inhibitions, relief of sexual monotony, improvement of sexual performance, and increased sexual interest in the spouse (Fang, 1976). Other positive aspects are implied in many of the motivations described before, and include such experiences as feeling loved and wanted, enhanced self-esteem, a sense of autonomy, personal growth, a revitalization of the marriage, and a renewed appreciation of the spouse.

Negative Aspects

Despite all of the positive aspects just mentioned, there are many problems associated with swinging and with conducting extramarital affairs, even among people who consider their own extramarital behavior morally justified.

1) Practical problems. The maintenance of secret affairs requires that one has to have a private place to meet, and that one has to be careful in telephoning, writing, and seeing the extramarital partner. Different types of practical problems are encountered in sexually open marriages. The following problems were mentioned by at least 50% of those sampled in a study by Ramey (1975): lack of time, scheduling difficulties, problems with babysitting, sleeping arrangements, housekeeping, and situational complexities. It seems quite likely that such problems can intensify due to the emotional conflicts surrounding the outside relationship. The main practical problems mentioned by swingers are the risk of venereal disease, and nowadays AIDS, and the difficulties in finding appropriate partners.

2) Emotional resistance. According to Hunt (1974), nearly everyone involved in extramarital relationships experiences fear, anxiety, and guilt feelings, although most overcome such feelings as time passes. Atwater (1979) also reports the existence of conflict, anxiety, and guilt among women involved in extramarital relationships. Furthermore, emotional problems are by no means absent among swingers. Many people who are, or have been, involved in swinging point to such factors as the lack of commitment and involvement, the mechanical and impersonal character of swinging, difficulties in finding appropriate partners, guilt, disillusionment and disappointment, boredom and loss of interest, fear of discovery, inability to live up to one's own psychosexual image, impotence, and the wife's inability to deal with the situation (Denfeld, 1974).

3) Jealousy. Most people in our society experience jealousy as a response to discovering that one's partner has fallen in love or become sexually involved with another person. Jealousy can include feelings of anger, despair, fear, resentment, and depression. It results primarily from the perception that the uniqueness, togetherness, and intimacy of the relationship has been violated. Jealousy is more prevalent among people who feel insecure about, and are very dependent upon, the relationship (Buunk and Bringle, 1987). The jealousy response is likely to be particularly intense when the partner's behavior is perceived as betrayal or unfaithfulness, but jealousy is by no means absent in persons who do not view extramarital sex in this way. For instance, only around 20% of the individuals in sexually open marriages claim that they are never jealous (Buunk, 1981; Ramey, 1975), and even this 20% may, at times, be jealous, but may label their feelings differently or deny this frequently condemned emotion. Furthermore, jealousy has been shown to constitute a problem among swingers (Bartell, 1971), although swingers are less jealous than nonswingers (Jenks, 1985b).

A longitudinal study of sexually open marriages, in which couples were reinterviewed five years after the first interview, sheds some light on the persistent nature as well as the changeability of jealousy (Buunk, 1987b). Despite the fact that some respondents felt they had been able to reduce their jealousy, the sample taken as a whole experienced an increase in jealousy. This is very striking because the people in this rather liberal sample had probably made numerous efforts to overcome their jealousy. However, this study offered no support for the assumption that jealousy is a stable personality characteristic: most individuals who were quite jealous during the second interview had not been five years before, and vice versa. Other research has shown that a lessened degree of jealousy over time was more apparent among those who had become less dependent upon, and more trusting of, their spouse. Being able to accept one's jealousy as well as constructive communication with the spouse seems to play a role in reducing jealousy (Buunk, 1981).

4) Threat to marriage. Many people seem to refrain from extramarital sex out of fear of its potential negative impact on their marriage. Indeed, extramarital relationships are often threatening to marriage, particularly since they can give rise to destructive, even violent conflicts (Buunk, 1986). But even without such conflicts, the marital relationship can become jeopardized. For instance, swingers sometimes point to the development of outside emotional involvements, despite their ground rules. In Buunk's (1980b) study of sexually open marriages, about one-fourth of the subjects reported that at certain moments their marriages had been threatened by their extramarital involvements. In Ramey's (1975) sample of similar marriages, daily tensions and pressures upon the primary relationship were mentioned by no less than 60%, indicating the potentially negative consequences upon one's marriage of even those outside relationships occurring with mutual consent.

On the other hand, positive effects upon marriage are claimed by many who have been involved in extramarital relationships. Thus Knapp (1976), on the basis of her study of sexually open marriages, maintains that, on the average, these unions had improved as a consequence of their outside relationships. In his sample, Hunt (1974, p. 200) reported that many of the currently married males and females involved in extramarital relationships believe that "their marriages have not been adversely affected, and a small number think that it has actually benefited their marital sex relationships." However, it seems likely that in this study and in comparable studies, the reports of the subjects are, as Hunt suggests, "sometimes an accurate assessment but that more often the individual who feels that his or her extramarital behavior has harmed nothing and perhaps done some good, is seeking to rationalize his behavior, or failing to perceive what's actually happening to the marriage."

Hunt's skeptical statement (1974) is relevant to much research on the positive effects of extramarital sex, especially for studies among people who have a value system favoring sexually non-exclusive marriages, as is underlined by the earlier mentioned longitudinal study on sexually open marriages (Buunk, 1987b). This study showed that in these marriages, over a five year period, the quality of the marital relationships had deteriorated considerably. Relational as well as sexual satisfaction had decreased substantially. Emotional dependency of the spouse had also lessened, possibly indicating that the respondents had turned away from their spouses. Thus, these data do not substantiate the idea that extramarital relationships are beneficial to the marital relationship. On the other hand, one cannot conclude from this study that the effects of outside relationships are disastrous to marriage, since it is possible that the disintegration of marital quality would have occurred anyhow. Given the age of the respondents in this sample, it is not completely unlikely that the findings discussed here reflect, at least partially, the decline of marital satisfaction over the life-cycle.

Extramarital relationships often play a role in the divorce process. In studies of divorced couples, extramarital relationships are consistently indicated as a frequent, although never the most frequent, reason for the divorce. For example, in a study by Ailsa Burns (1984), 31% of the divorcé(e)s mentioned the husband's association with another woman as cause of the breakdown of the marriage. It is difficult, however, if not impossible, to draw from this type of research any conclusions about the consequences of extramarital relationships upon the stability of marriages, especially since we do not know how many, and which couples, remain together despite an extramarital affair. In this regard, Hunt's (1974) data are interesting. He found that divorced men had started extramarital relationships much earlier in their marriage than still-married men with extramarital experience. As Hunt points out, this could be the result either of the early recognition that the marriage was a hopeless mistake, or of neurotic traits that would have damaged the marriage anyhow—but in both cases it is not the extramarital activity itself that is the ultimate cause of divorce. Hunt's conclusions seem quite compatible with the finding of Graham Spanier and Randie Margolis (1983). Nearly 40% of their sample of 205 divorces had been involved in extramarital affairs. Nevertheless, most respondents felt their extramarital affairs were a consequence, rather than a cause, of their marital problems and that the majority of affairs had begun in the first four years of the marriage.

A study by Buunk (1987a) provides some illuminating data on the causal conditions under which extramarital affairs may lead to divorce. This study compared a group of men and women who had all been sexually involved outside their marital or cohabiting relationship and who had since broken up, with a matched control group of people who also had been involved in such outside relationships, but were still living with their primary partner. The results indicated that, compared to the control group, the breakup group reported: 1) a significantly higher level of relational dissatisfaction, which had led to extramarital affairs, and at the same time, 2) a stronger disapproval of extramarital sex. However, the two groups did not differ in the number of extradyadic relationships, and the degree of involvement in these relationships.

Stability of Extramarital Behavior Patterns

It is not quite clear to what extent extramarital activity is a recurrent and stable pattern, rather than an incidental and unstable one. Atwater (1979) found that most (62%) of the women she interviewed established patterns of repeated extramarital sex with other partners after the relationship with their first partner had ended. The majority of this group had had two to six partners, with the average length of a relationship being one year. On the other hand, the study by Anthony Pietropinto and Jacqueline Simenauer (1977) showed that most of the men with extramarital experience had had only one or two relationships, although, of course, these relationships could have continued over a considerable period of time. In any case, a large majority of adulterous men and women have not had more than five affairs (Athanasiou et al., 1970).

There are also little data available regarding the stability of swinging as a lifestyle. We do not know the percentage of couples that, after initially trying it, quit swinging, and how long the remaining couples continued their practice. However, given the fact that so few Americans ever try swinging, the fact that many counselors have seen couples who dropped out of swinging and the fact that, of course, not all dropouts go see a counselor, it seems quite likely that there is only a very small group of committed swinging couples who continue their behavior over a number of years. The main reasons to drop out of swinging tend to be: jealousy, guilt, threat to marriage, development of attachment to other partners, and boredom (Denfeld, 1974). However, these reasons may be typical for couples who sought counseling during or after their swinging activities. A study by Bernard Murstein and his colleagues (Murstein, Case, and Gunn, 1985) showed that, according to ex-swingers themselves, none of these reasons is of particular significance. Instead, it appeared that in many respects ex-swinger wives were clearly more conventional than swinging wives, while the husbands in both groups hardly differed from one another. According to both husbands and wives, the wife was primarily responsible for discontinuing swinging activities. Indeed, the main reason mentioned for quitting the swinging scene was the wife's inability to deal with such a lifestyle. The ex-swingers also pointed to monetary considerations, mentioned the time-consuming nature of the activity, and expressed dissatisfaction with the quality of partners. Recently, fear of contracting AIDS is probably an important reason to quit swinging.

More is known about the persistence of sexually open marriages, since some longitudinal studies are available with respect to this lifestyle. However, the data on this issue seem somewhat contradictory. Arlene Rubin and James Adams (1986) found that only two couples of their original sample of twenty-three couples with sexually open marriages had returned to a sexually exclusive lifestyle five years later. On the other hand, Mary Ann Watson (1981), who contacted nineteen married couples involved in sexually open marriages two years after an initial interview, found that all couples except for one had returned to monogamous relationships with their spouses. The longitudinal study by Bram Buunk (1987b) seems to reconcile these seemingly incompatible findings. This study showed that compared to five years earlier, the sample as whole was somewhat less inclined to engage in extramarital sexual behavior, particularly long-term affairs. However, the majority was still in favor of incidental extramarital contacts.

REVIEW QUESTIONS

1) Which factors are related to extramarital attitudes and behavior?
2) What is the difference between excuse and justification? How is this related to different types of extramarital relations?
3) What can be said about the effects of extramarital affairs upon marriage?

SUGGESTED PROJECTS

1) Interview a police officer on the reasons for violent marital conflicts, and establish how often extramarital relationships play a role.
2) Interview couples on how they feel about extramarital affairs, under what circumstances they themselves would become involved, and how they would react if their spouses were to do so.
3) Find a magazine published by a swinging club and analyze the contact ads. Which characteristics are looked for in other couples? What characteristics are presented?

CHAPTER
6

Communal Groups

DEFINING COMMUNAL GROUPS

THE PRESENTATION OF A totally unambiguous definition of communes which allows us to distinguish them perfectly from other lifestyle arrangements is a difficult, if not impossible, chore. One of the compounding factors is the large variety of communal-type groups and the array of terms used to describe them: cooperatives, cooperative households, utopian communities, communes, collectives, intentional communities, experimental communities, shared households, group marriages, and alternative families are all terms used to denote a type of living arrangement that is often presented as an alternative to the traditional nuclear family. Nevertheless, all such arrangements do have some common elements.

One of the most useful working definitions of communes, offered by Benjamin Zablocki (1980, p. 7), covers most of these: "any group of five or more adult individuals (plus children if any), the majority of whose dyads are not cemented by blood or marriage, who have decided to live together, without compulsion, focused upon the achievement of community, for which a collective household is deemed essential."

In general, we agree with this definition, although it seems justifiable to also include groups that only have three or four members (Fairfield, 1972). A crucial element contained in Zablocki's (1980) definition is that the commune is not entirely composed of related individuals. This needs to be emphasized because it creates a distinction between a commune and an extended family system, where kinship or marriage relations are the social cement of the group.

It was from one of the books that I copied out the bylaws of the village, which, it turned out, went by the official name of Manerva Nueva, Incorporated. These are the village's bylaws, all 10 of them.

1) Membership is open to anyone on the Planet Earth. Access is denied no one.

2) There is one class of membership: first class or full member.

3) All property is and shall be held in common by all members.

4) Any member attending a meeting is entitled to equal voting rights with all members in attendance.

5) Annual meetings begin at sunrise July 4 of each year and continue until agreement on all issues under discussion is reached.

6) Any member may declare any question an important one which then can be acted upon only after meditation and consultation of the I CHING, an oracle.

7) All funds received by the corporation shall be held for use for all by Treasurers appointed by the Board of Directors.

8) Meetings may be called by any member or director upon notification of other members within a reasonable time prior to the holding of said meeting.

9) All major decisions must be made in agreement with the I CHING. Any issue may be declared a major issue by any member.

10) Individual members living in communities operated by Manerva Nueva may not hold private funds or property (personal belongings and effects excepted).

Figure 6.1 The bylaws of Manerva Nueva closely fit the image that many people have of communes

Source: Fairfield (1972).

SOCIETAL CONTEXT

Incidence in Society

Although many Americans probably associate communes primarily with the counterculture, hippie movement, drugscene, and sexual revolution of the late 1960s, communalism is by no means a recent phenomenon. As John Bennett (1975, p. 63) noted, communes are "the oldest 'new' and the most traditional 'experimental' social movement in the West." We find a desire to abolish the family and replace it with a more communal arrangement as far back as in Plato's *Republic*. Zablocki (1980) locates the earliest period of communalism during the Roman Empire as between 100 BC and AD 100. These were sectarian responses to the threat of an impinging Roman culture. The original Christian communities that arose during the first century were also communal in nature. In the past few centuries we have witnessed the recurrent rise and decline of numerous communal movements, particularly in times of cultural crises. Some, like the Shakers, the Harmonists, and the Ephrataites, lasted a century or more. Most, however, were very temporary experiments. Rosabeth Moss Kanter (1972) distinguished three historical waves of communalism in the U.S.: a period before 1845 when religious themes were central; a period in the 1840s when economic and political issues were central; and the most recent psychosocial period that emerged in the 1960s when there was a severe erosion of faith in American institutions due to, among other things, the civil rights struggle and the Vietnam War. Since the early 1970s, however, there has been a decline in the number of newly formed communes.

Communal arrangements have never attracted more than a tiny minority of the population. The number of communal experiments in American society since 1820 has constantly vacillated between approximately 15 and 60 per each five-year period. From 1965–1970, however, this number exploded tremendously to several thousands. Furthermore, while almost all nineteenth century communes were rural, it is estimated that in 1970 there were roughly one thousand rural communes in North America and at least twice as many urban ones. It needs to be pointed out that the number of communes does not tell us how many individuals have actually become involved in communal lifestyles. Prior to the nineteenth century, communes tended to have over 100 adult members. This number dropped to between 50 and 100 until the peak in the last few decades, when the average urban commune consisted of 11 members and the average rural commune had just under 40 members. Given these relatively small sizes, it can be estimated that not more than 250,000 persons lived in communes in 1980, only one-tenth of a percent of the total U.S. population (Zablocki, 1980), and there is no reason to assume that this figure is higher today. Also, despite the overwhelming media exposure of communes associated with new religious movements, such as Hare Krishna and the Unification Church, less than 10,000 (young) people presently live in such groups (Richardson, 1983).

In other Western countries there is an even smaller incidence of communal groups than in the United States. Harrie Jansen (1980), who collected data on communes in the Netherlands, was, after considerable effort, only able to locate seventy-two groups in the beginning of the 1970s. The size of most communes was also considerably smaller than in the United States, 6.3 members per group. This duplicates findings in Denmark, another highly industrialized society with a large number of especially urban communes (Shey, 1977). Recently, in the Netherlands, some novel types of communes have come to be called living groups — a more neutral term referring to a group of people who live together, but do not necessarily have common ideological goals. The number of such groups has been estimated to be as high as 7000 (Buunk,1983).

The typical living group consists of four to six persons (with or without children) who do not have sexual relations with one another and are economically independent to a large extent, yet share various tasks in the common household (Weggemans et al., 1985). Though each member is expected to have individual financial resources and can spend earnings without group consent, a certain amount of money is collectively reserved to pay for the rent, electricity, food, furniture, etc. All members contribute to the collective fund.

Attitudes in Society

The prevalent societal attitude toward communal groups has been one of ambivalence. The more these groups adhere to the dominant norms and values of society, the smaller the chance that they will be labelled "deviant," "dangerous," "threatening," or "morally objectionable." Neighbors, citizen committees, organized religions, and other groups that have perceived their interests to be threatened have been especially overtly antagonistic toward communes. Arson, beatings, bombings, and other forms of harassment have been commonplace throughout recent history.

Raymond Muncy (1988) points out that in nineteenth century America, communal experiments, unless celibacy was practiced, were considered a threat to the sacred institution of monogamous marriage. Communes questioned and offered alternatives to accepted family patterns in many ways: child-rearing, property ownership, economic arrangements, and sexual relations to mention a few. At a time when any sexual relationship outside marriage was branded as sinful and intolerable by the still extremely powerful churches, and the state concurred by making such behavior illegal, numerous communal movements faced severe organized opposition.

Although public agencies in the 1970s and 1980s have occasionally raided communes or otherwise forced them to disband, they have usually been quite hesitant to become involved. American law has repeatedly affirmed the rights of communes to exist and various decisions that support the civil rights of communards have been handed down by the courts.

In some (more liberal) places in the United States, present-day communes that have managed to survive for a lengthy period of time (over a decade) and their members have been fairly easily absorbed into the larger community. Bennett Berger (1988), who has followed the development of communal groups along the northern California coast, notes that as commune members gradually blend in with the local population it is increasingly difficult to distinguish commune members from noncommune members. In fact they have become what Bennett Berger calls "stable 'old' residents": established fellow citizens who have actively committed themselves to maintaining and improving the region's welfare. Nevertheless, it is doubtful whether such insertion into local mainstream society is possible anywhere but in the most tolerant geographical areas of the United States.

A large segment of the population still clearly disapproves of communal living. In the early seventies a national study of attitudes toward various social movements showed that approximately 20% of the American population was willing to accept and tolerate communal arrangements (Yankelovich, 1974). The proportion interested in practicing such a lifestyle was much lower, also among college students. One study found that 16% of college students had an interest in living communally while group marriage (a type of commune in which multiple, sexual relationships existed) was even less appreciated; here a mere 5% would seriously be willing to consider such an arrangement for themselves (Edwards and Stinnet, 1974). If anything, these figures are probably even lower today.

American society has been especially hostile toward such communal arrangements as polygamy and the communally-oriented new religious movements (or, more popularly, cults). This is evidenced by fines, lawsuits, official investigations, raids, and violence. While polygamy was a heated issue during the nineteenth century, today it is the demands that the new religious movements make on their members that evoke serious opposition. Communal rituals and practices such as mass wedding ceremonies, the surrendering of all personal belongings, the members' focus on the group as a new family, breaking of ties with outsiders, and the total dedication to the group, has led many concerned parents and sympathetic others to lobby against these so-called "destructive cults." Recent studies reveal that the American public is willing to go to great lengths to stop such groups from spreading (McClosky and Brill, 1983; Richardson and Van Driel, 1984). A 1987 Gallup poll showed that members of "cults" are the least desired neighbors of the American public.

As with other alternative lifestyles, research has shown that the Dutch tend to be more appreciative of communal groups. Even here, however, there is a considerable amount of disapproval. Data from the 1985 Dutch National Social and Cultural Bureau show that 41% of the Dutch population disapprove of communal living arrangements. Attraction to such a lifestyle is even lower: a large 1985 survey (conducted 1986) in the Netherlands revealed that only a few percent of high school students would consider living communally. As they are basically a rather collectivistic type of arrangement, it seems unlikely that communal arrangements will ever attract a substantial part of the population in Western countries, given the individualistic value patterns in these countries.

VARIETIES OF THE COMMUNAL LIFE

There is an enormous diversity in types of communes with respect to variables such as sexual and ethnic composition, size, ideology, organizational form, and geographic location. Because communes can differ on a myriad of dimensions, it has been very difficult to reach a consensus on how to best differentiate one type of commune from another. If we do not distinguish between various types of communes, and simply treat them all as if they were all the same we run the risk of missing important distinctions and drowning in a sea of information. Two often-used classification systems are those proposed by Richard Fairfield (1972) and Zablocki (1980), and we will discuss both typologies briefly here.

Fairfield (1972) used a rough, atheoretical typology of six different sorts of communes.

1. *Religious communes:* Traditionally these include mainly the rural and agricultural Christian communes; since the end of the sixties more communes with an Eastern religion, such as Buddhist and Hindu communes, have emerged.

2. *Ideological communes:* Groups that try to live according to a secular rationalistic philosophy such as Marxism, feminism, or radical behaviorism.

3. *Hippie communes:* Groups typical of the late 1960s, with an emphasis on experience and mysticism, expressed, for instance, in the use of drugs.

4. *Service communes:* Help-oriented or therapeutic groups created to provide a work and recreational environment for disadvantaged persons.

5. *Youth communes:* Usually groups of college graduates who share the advantages of group living, similar to the Dutch living groups discussed earlier.

6. *Group marriages:* Groups mostly consisting of two women and a man, or two couples that consider themselves married to one another, and where all participants have an intimate, sexual relationship with at least two others.

Another often-cited classification scheme is that presented by Zablocki (1980) in his already classic book *Alienation and Charisma.* He developed a typology based on two dimensions: 1) whether commune members focus on changing themselves or changing society ("a strategy of consciousness versus direct action" in Zablocki's terms); and 2) whether the focus of attention is the spiritual world, the individual self, the commune, or secular society. The subdivisions within these two dimensions led to an eight-fold typology of communes that is shown in Table 6.1. The following can be said about these types of communal lifestyles.

1. *Eastern communes:* The beliefs of these groups are derived from an Eastern religious tradition.

2. *Christian communes:* The beliefs of these groups revolve around Western traditions of Christianity.

3. *Psychological communes:* These are primarily concerned with psychological growth, consciousness raising, and self-actualization. The communal environment is meant to create a setting that fosters these processes.

4. *Rehabilitational communes:* Action-oriented groups that exist to heal, cure, or repair individuals who have psychological problems and who cannot solve them individually.

5. *Cooperative communes:* The focus here is on the cooperative nature of man and his social being. Members attempt to create a loosely-structured, loosely-planned, harmonious collective community.

6. *Alternative family communes:* A deliberate attempt is made to create a new form of living in which a kind of extended family constellation is envisioned.

7. *Countercultural commune:* The group has as a goal to change society and embraces a set of beliefs and behaviors that carry with them a clear rejection of the traditions and institutions of mainstream society.

8. *Political communes:* A major goal is to transform society and its (political) institutions. Society, as such, is rejected, based on a secular ideological philosophy, and efforts are made to influence the political edifice of society.

Table 6.1 Eight Types of Commune Ideologies

Locus of Attention	Strategic Philosophy	
	Consciousness	Direct Action
Spiritual World	Eastern	Christian
Individual Self	Psychological	Rehabilitational
Primary Group / Community	Cooperative	Alternative Family
Secular Society	Countercultural	Political

Source: Zablocki (1980), p. 204.

The typologies of Fairfield (1972) and Zablocki (1980) differ in many ways. Fairfield, for instance, reserves an entire category for the phenomenon of group marriage while Zablocki considers it only one of several types of "alternative families." Neither typology is correct or incorrect. Their value depends on what aspect of communal life one is interested in. One important distinction that is missing in both typologies, however, is the contrast *urban-rural*. Rural communes have often been considered to be quite distinct because they tend to be larger, more isolated, and demand higher levels of commitment from their members. These communes generally constitute a kind of subsociety and are more self-sufficient and isolated than urban communes. Members often own and share one or more dwellings (usually a farm) on a relatively large piece of land, and can provide many daily needs by growing crops and engaging in animal husbandry. Urban communes, on the other hand, which are a much more recent phenomenon, exist within the confines of a city environment and are adapted to it. A good deal of income is accumulated through employment outside the commune, while the members have many contacts in the outside world and participate in this world. A single house, originally meant for a nuclear family unit, is large enough to accommodate these individuals. Because of the close connection urban communes have with the activities of the outside world, and their less radical departure from society, authors like Bennett Berger and his associates (1972) consider this type of group to be a less pure form of commune than the rural type.

A special type of communal arrangement is found among senior citizens. In contrast to the publicity prone contemporary retirement communities (usually situated in the sun-belt states), where recreational activities and leisure are a central focus, senior citizen communal arrangements are more far-reaching. Gordon Streib and Mary Hilker (1980) describe the "Share-A-Home" project where a group of elderly persons share a house with a paid staff to take care of all domestic duties. Most of those involved are no longer capable of performing all the tasks necessary for daily living. Living together with others is not only cheaper than a nursing home but also frees the individual from the burden of housekeeping. Furthermore, it offers a family of caring peers who care about and support each other, and allows the person to keep a substantial degree of autonomy and independence.

Various communes with members of all ages, such as the kibbutzim, allow the elderly to continue functioning as valuable members of the group, while gradually reducing the workload and responsibilities of those growing older. Many problems of the elderly in modern society are thus obviated, especially the feelings of being useless and lonely.

CHARACTERISTICS OF COMMUNE MEMBERS

Though commune members vary widely with respect to variables such as race, sex, age, and education, certain patterns can be delineated.

1) Ethnicity. Several studies have revealed that communalism is a white man's variant lifestyle. In Zablocki's (1980) study, more than three-quarters of the 120 communes he examined consisted of an entirely white population. In total, less than 1% of the members in his sample were black, as opposed to 11% of the United States' population. Black males especially have objections to communal life. A recent study showed that white males were much more in favor of communes than were black males, with females of both races holding an intermediate position (Erickson, 1980).

2) Religion. Commune membership is not only related to ethnicity, but also to religion. Protestants are under-represented, while Jews are over-represented — possibly stimulated by the Kibbutz movement in Israel. Religion is still an important theme for most communards. A recent nationwide longitudinal study of urban communes (Aidala, 1984) revealed that almost 90% of commune members, regardless of the type of commune in which they resided, had experimented with religion — by joining a religious movement, for example.

3) Social background. In several ways commune members resemble mainstream America much more than is generally supposed. In the first place, communes are not exclusively a middle-class phenomenon. The percentage of people claiming a middle-class background matches that for the total United States' population. Perhaps more surprising is the fact that the family of origin of communards is not typically a broken home or an otherwise malfunctioning social unit. On the contrary, most members come from close-knit, intact families (90% intact versus 78% for the total population). These home environments are generally experienced to have been very personal and affectionate places (Zablocki, 1980).

4) Marital status. Most communards are young singles. Zablocki (1980) found that 72% of his respondents had never been married and that 80% did not have children. About 78% of his respondents in urban communes and 50% of those in rural communes had joined before the age of 30. Most participants in group marriages are also younger than 30 (Constantine and Constantine, 1973).

5) Lifestyle and political views. Although, politically speaking, communards tend to lean to the left, this political activism tends to decrease upon joining the commune. Zablocki (1980), for example, found that 22% of communards had participated in riots before joining a commune, 57% in anti-war demonstrations, and 33% in civil rights demonstrations; these percentages decreased to respectively 3%, 9%, and 6% after joining. James Richardson (1983) reports on a study of a Jesus Movement communal group in a rural setting that showed a large increase in political apathy. Though a significant segment of the group indicated they were either liberal or radical before joining, only a few held on to their political convictions afterwards. Not only is political activism changed by commune membership, drug use is also dampened. In Zablocki's (1980) sample, close to 83% had used drugs prior to membership, but this dropped to 44% afterwards. The decrease was especially striking among Eastern religious groups (96.4% to 16.1%), Christian groups (56.2% to 8.8%), and rehabilitational groups (63.2% to 5.3%).

6) Personality. Communards seem to possess some specific personality characteristics that can probably best be summarized as an orientation toward change and self-fulfillment. It has been found that communards are more likely to value the here and now, espouse egalitarian and emancipatory values, seek a more meaningful life, be disillusioned with society, be religious experimenters, and be estranged from the capitalist work ethic. In a large scale review of the numerous psychological and psychiatric studies of members of new religious movements, James Richardson (1985) found that these individuals scored quite similarly to other individuals of the same age on a variety of psychological tests. However, religious commune members were more self-aware, more dependent, and less stressful than their peers.

7) Age. Communalism has been associated with youth, and commune-living envisioned as an intermediate station between childhood and adulthood. A quick glance at the age composition of contemporary communes reveals that there is some truth to this common view. Nevertheless, a historical review of "utopian" communities by Shalamit Reinharz (1988) shows that this has definitely not always been the case. Some communes have proved to be especially attractive to the elderly, while most have had members of various ages. Especially the few highly successful communes of the past, like the Oneida, needed to address the age and aging issue, since young members who remained in the group eventually grew old. The same applies to the long-term commune members who opted for a communal lifestyle in the sixties. They are now headed for middle age. Consequently, as in the Israeli kibbutzim, groups that initially started out as homogeneous youth groups become transformed into multigenerational extended "family" structures.

JOINING AND LEAVING COMMUNES

Motivations

Different motivations can lie behind the decision to join or start a commune. For instance, depending upon the type of commune, religious, political, sexual, relational, or idealistic motives may be predominant. For some members their lifestyle is a way to put highly valued ideals into practice, i.e., ideals concerning the eradication of private property, sex role equality, nonexclusive love, personal growth, or religious devotion. Others, those involved in group marriages, for example, primarily look for more companionship, a variety of sexual partners, the emergence of different aspects of personality, feeling more desired and wanted, and personal growth and fulfillment (Constantine and Constantine, 1973). Still others, such as senior citizens, look for a combination of social and instrumental support.

Zablocki (1980) notes that communards mention ideological reasons most often as the reason to join a commune. This applies for both members of urban and rural communes, and especially for those who elect to join a religious group. Personal reasons, such as escaping loneliness, improving interpersonal skills, and experiencing a new lifestyle are the second most often-mentioned motive, though more predominant among members of secular groups. Two other often-mentioned motives are relational and convenience. Relational motives, such as joining friends, family, or loved-ones, are also most characteristic of those who enter secular groups. In a study of Dutch communes, Jansen (1980) found that relational self-actualization was actually the most important reason to stay in communes. This included developing true and open relationships, being corrected by others' criticism, and becoming more open and honest. Convenience or pragmatic motives, including economic advantages, childcare arrangements, and the nice location of the commune, are especially mentioned by joiners of secular urban communes.

Although communes among the elderly have been described in the literature, it is important to realize that most individuals join communes at a stage in their life-cycle when they are dealing with their self-identity and are on the brink of stepping out from underneath their parents' protective wings into the "real" world (Erikson, 1963). Communes play a role in the transition from the sheltered life led in one's parents' home to participation in the outside world, thus between youth roles and adult roles. Communes help to bridge this gap by offering affection, security, a sense of belonging and identity, and by performing various therapeutic and problem-solving functions. Before communards make the decision to join a commune they are often faced with identity problems, tend to experience "mainstream existence" as rather meaningless, and become extremely aware that some kind of void needs to be filled. They become "seekers" and sometimes explicitly label themselves as such (Straus, 1976). Seekership is a widespread phenomenon among contemporary youth and denotes a quest for meaning and meaningful relationships in life. Indicative of this seekership is that 90% of commune members leave within two years (Levine, 1984) and that many communards subsequently resume the search for fulfillment in another communal group. Some 20% of the communards in Zablocki's (1980) study left their original group and joined another commune within a year. Richardson (1978) comments that many individuals in religious communal movements make the move from one group to another several times, a behavior he labels "conversion careers." Of course, individuals with a religious world view and a religious problem-solving perspective will be more likely to experiment with religious communes. Moving from one commune to another does not imply that "once a communard, always a communard." As a matter of fact, most individuals eventually return to mainstream society and assume societally accepted roles, a reentry into conventional life that is usually fairly easy (Zablocki, 1980).

The search for a sense of community is one motive that seems to clearly distinguish communes from lifestyles such as singlehood, non-marital cohabitation, and sexually open marriages. Some sociologists have suggested that mass society has become so devoid of affectivity and so instrumental and impersonal that the urge for a sense of community has become very profound for large segments of modern day youth (Richardson et al., 1978). Indeed, surveys indicate that in the 1970s, the percentage of Americans that experienced a "hungering for community" grew from 32% in 1973 to 47% in 1980 (Yankelovich, 1982). However, such a hungering seems at odds with the predominantly individualistic value pattern now pervasive in society. Indeed, although entering a commune represents a rejection of this individualistic pattern, it is clear that individuals who join communes are foremost interested in what communes can offer them in the process of self-discovery. As Zablocki (1980) has noted, it is very difficult for individuals brought up in present-day society to surrender their own needs and wishes for the sake of the group. Due to the ubiquitous individualistic orientation of the communards, they seldom become or remain highly committed to the group. Seen in this light it is hardly surprising to see so many individuals constantly moving in and out of such groups. This appears to be especially true for urban communes, where individuals embrace values more akin to modern society. Rural communes are somewhat more stable. One of the reasons lies in the claim by Berger and his colleagues that such communes function more as a real family and define themselves more in terms of a family (Berger, Hackett, & Millar, 1972).

Joining the Commune

Various models have been advanced to account for the actual process of absorbing new members into communal type movements (e.g., Zablocki, 1980; Lofland and Stark, 1965). In general, there is either a focus on 1) predisposing factors, such as needs and frustrations of individuals; or 2) situational factors, such as accidentally meeting a group at the "right moment"; or 3) recruitment strategies of the communes to attract new members; or 4) socioaffective relations between the individual and the group (or members of the group) through interaction and a loosening of ties with outsiders (friends, relatives). Several authors have noticed that all of these foci treat the novice as a rather passive human being, constantly being pushed and pulled by factors out of his/her reach. It is more fruitful, however, to view the individual not as an object that is simply more or less vulnerable to becoming a commune member, but as an active agent seeking to create a meaningful life in interaction with other individuals and outside agencies (Straus, 1976; Richardson, 1985).

According to Straus (1976), joining a commune is basically a process of experimentation. At some point in the search for a variant lifestyle an individual makes contact with a communal group that seems to offer something. Both the group and the potential recruit enter a process of negotiation — what can the other mean for me? If the potential recruit is really interested, he or she will start "checking out" the group. This occurs, among other things, by attending meetings, observing group activities, and talking to members. The next phase is "trying out." One gets involved in day to day activities and begins to function as a member. If all goes well, commitment to the group follows. Oftentimes the verdict is negative; only one out of five-hundred youngsters who are approached by proselytizing communal movements ever actually join (Levine, 1984). Also, the commune does not always make the joining process easy. Many communes have membership requirements that limit the number of individuals who can join.

The typical communard goes through various stages between entering and leaving the communal group. Roger Straus (1976) distinguishes two important and distinct chronological phases. First, there is the "redhot phase" in which the novice is heavily committed and dedicated to the group in a sometimes exaggerated way. The emotions involved resemble falling in love. As in other relationship forms, the romance does not last long. Straus speaks of "transition to maintenance," a settling down within the group and a decrease in fervent behavior. The communard is now ready for coping with the reality of functioning in a communal setting.

Leaving the Commune

Most members leave the group in an early stage: half of Zablocki's sample (1980) left before the end of their first year and only 32% sat out two entire years. It appears that after the initial high levels of dedication and intense participation wear off, members often become disenchanted. Leaving a commune can take place in the following four different ways:

1) Exiting. This is the most common manner of disaffiliation. The pushes and pulls of communal life and life outside the commune exert influence on the individual, and both are equally important causes, according to Zablocki (1980), for individuals to leave. The major reasons for growing discontentment and disaffiliation are relational and ideological. Relational problems can refer to relationships with commune members or outsiders. If relationships with outsiders are valued positively and/or relationships with insiders negatively, one will develop a propensity to leave the commune. Ideological reasons may deal with issues such as a discovery that the groups' ideology does not match one's own, a desire for something different, or discovery of inconsistencies in the group's ideological stance. Leaving a group in which high levels of commitment exist, and in which strict recruitment criteria are employed, is more difficult because of the relatively strong ties with other members and the various investments the individual has made in the group. In such groups there is also often a great deal of pressure from within the group not to leave.

2) Expulsion. Expulsion (or excommunication) occurs far less. Only 2% of Zablocki's (1980) sample of leavers had left by means of expulsion. Most groups have either formal or informal guidelines that determine when and how a member should be removed. The Unification Church, for instance, has repeatedly removed individuals who were considered to be psychologically unstable.

3) Discontinuation. In 15% of Zablocki's sample of leavers, the reason for leaving was simply that the commune had ceased to exist. Of course, the smaller the commune, the larger the chance that this will occur. One member or one couple leaving a group of five can have severe consequences for the commune's viability.

4) Extraction. There are sometimes outsiders who attempt to extract the member from the commune. In most instances extraction is non-coercive. The communard is convinced and persuaded that he or she should leave. This process partially overlaps that of what we have called exiting. Another type of extraction is coercive extraction. During the past decade thousands of members of religious communes have been coercively usurped from their groups and subsequently "de-programmed." The goal of this extreme measure is to instill more acceptable forms of beliefs and behaviors in ex-members (Shupe and Bromley, 1980).

Most departures tend to be rather painless because of low levels of commitment and the short stay in the commune. The more committed one was, the more likely it is that leaving will be painful. Following disaffiliation there is a time when the ex-member must cope with life without the group. This often resembles a process of mourning (Levine, 1984). Nevertheless, most ex-members positively evaluate their past experiences in a commune.

Disaffiliation can also leave deep emotional scars. According to Saul Levine (1984), those who do not leave on a voluntarily basis (especially if they are "deprogrammed") are often incapable of resolving their conflicts and problems. The natural rhythm of leaving and mourning is radically disturbed, and it is difficult for the individuals concerned to cope effectively with their past actions and experiences, and to put them into perspective.

POSITIVE AND NEGATIVE ASPECTS
OF COMMUNAL LIVING

In many ways, communal living can be a rewarding experience, especially for young adults, who may find security, a sense of identity, and an opportunity to experiment in a variant lifestyle before fully entering society. However, partially due to the oftentimes high expec-tations and idealistic goals, many problems may arise within commu-nes. We will now review some of the major areas where communal life offers specific costs and/or benefits.

Privacy and Freedom

Most outsiders consider lack of privacy the major obstacle to a satisfying life in a commune. In most groups, however, this is not the major complaint of members, although "some privacy in the midst of strong group contact seems essential for success" (Cornfield, 1983, p. 118). Remarkably, in many communes the members even complain that there is too much privacy and too little togetherness (Jansen, 1980). Furthermore, satisfied members mention their increased freedom as a major advantage of communal life. They are far less occupied with fixed work roles, rotate and share household duties; and partners indicate that they are less dependent on each other in emotional, economic, social, and sometimes sexual areas.

Gender Roles

Many communes are set up to institute more egalitarian domestic roles for males and females. This is usually considered to be a major advantage of communes. In many cases, however, communes fall far short of the goals of female liberation and an egalitarian division of labor. In Zablocki's (1980) study, for example, women spent much more time than men performing traditional female tasks such as cleaning, cooking, and taking care of the children. Female tasks, as in mainstream society, were also assigned lower status, as were females themselves.

A study by Leigh Minturn (1984) of six communes in Colorado also revealed that men and women in communes have different role expectations, which parallel traditional gender-related roles. Though more commune residents reported doing cross-gender chores than a selected sample of college students, this type of behavior was not frequently engaged in by either group (one-third of the communards versus one-fourth of the students).

Group marriages are also beset by male dominance. Data from a study of group marriages (Constantine and Constantine, 1973) for instance, show that of the 64 groups consisting of one married couple plus a single individual, only 1 group was comprised of one female and two males. All the others consisted of one male and two females.

It is also noteworthy that the Israeli kibbutzim, where every effort has been made to promote gender role equality, have tragically failed in this respect. At the present time males and females are once more engaged in tasks that reflect the traditional division of labor (Ben-Rafaël and Weitzman, 1984).

Somewhat more successful in this regard are the Dutch living groups we mentioned earlier. These modern communal groups are the result of two parallel societal developments, according to Saskia Poldervaart (in Weggemans et al., 1985): changing attitudes toward the family as an institution and thus the acceptance of other lifestyles as legitimate; and the growth of second-wave feminism. Especially this feminism has had a considerable impact on the rise of living groups. As a consequence, more than twice the number of women participate in living groups than in earlier and more traditional communal groups. Furthermore, men and women are expected to rotate all tasks. Though it is too early to tell whether Dutch living groups will be more successful at changing gender-roles than the Israeli kibbutzim, the fact that Dutch males are generally more willing to adopt female roles in the household can facilitate success in this area.

Sexual Exclusivity

Contrary to popular opinion, and as can be seen from Table 6.2, only a minority of communes endorse sexually nonexclusive partnerships, such as shifting sexual relationships or group marriages. However, the opposite attitude towards sexuality — celibacy — is found in an even smaller percentage of communes. The dominant pattern is either official or unofficial monogamy (Zablocki, 1980). Monogamy serves a purpose in communes: it can provide stability by circumventing rivalry, jealousy, and other negative feelings that surface in groups that advocate multiple sexual contacts within the group, such as the group marriage arrangements discussed by Larry and Joan Constantine (1973).

With the AIDS crisis at hand, and the rapid turnover of commune members, monogamy is becoming the guideline for ever more communes in the late 1980s. It appears that, at the moment, explicit dyads are being formed in already existing communes. Those communes, on the other hand, which strongly endorse sexual freedom are reverting to other coping strategies such as totally prohibiting sexual relations with outsiders, while limiting new membership. Because such initiatives basically run against the ideological tenets of various "free-sex" groups, tensions can build up which make dissolution more likely.

Despite the preference for monogamy in most communes, support for a traditional type of marital arrangement within the group is limited. Members indicate that the state of marriage should not prevent the development of close relationships with others, should not imply the adoption of traditional sex-role patterns, and should not result in strong emotional property claims on the partner (Jansen, 1980).

Group Interaction

It is often stated by those in favor of communes that self-growth, through interaction with multiple individuals and the group, is enhanced. The group is supposed to provide a secure social surrounding in which the individual can experience affection from various others and become immersed in a loving community environment. Hence, a feeling of "togetherness" can be obtained. However, this sketch is not always an accurate reflection of how communal life is experienced. The

Table 6.2 Sexual Organization of Rural and Urban Communes

Dominant Norms	Total % of Total
Compulsory celibacy	7
Voluntary celibacy	6
Licensed monogamy	
Commune approval required	5
Commune approval not required	17
Unofficial monogamy	
Marriage with commitment	25
Shifting sexual relationships	19
Partial group marriage	12
Group marriage, all included	1
Mixed	8
Total	100

Adapted from: Zablocki (1980), p. 339.

group orientation and intensive interaction of many communes that for some produce the idyllic picture painted above can also exacerbate strife and cause all kinds of conflicts and frictions, which can eventually lead to the attrition of members and the dissolution of the commune.

Group processes may have consequences for couples that join communes. Jealousy, envy, and conflicts of loyalty make couple relationships very fragile. In Zablocki's (1980) study, a large majority of legally married couples had either left the group or had separated at year's end. Part of this has to do with the fact that some couples join a commune to save a marriage. Dennis Jaffe and Rosabeth Moss Kanter (1977) found, however, that communal living often led to a development that can threaten dyads: a defusing of couple identity and reduced couple dependency. In addition, it was found that singlehood became a more viable option. These and other factors contributed to the instability of marriages in a communal setting.

Therapeutic Function

We have already mentioned that communes can fulfill an integrative function in the lives of members. Richardson (1985, p. 221) states that "the personality assessment data from studies of members reveals that life in the new religions is often therapeutic instead of harmful." In this sense, it is even useful to label some groups, especially those focused on rehabilitation, "therapeutic communities." The following therapeutic effects have been found: reduced neurotic distress and anxiety, increased self-esteem, self-actualization, suicide prevention, decreased anomie, termination of drug use, decreased psychosomatic symptoms, ego-clarification, renewed interest in family and community, increased concern for others, reduced fear of death, reduced criminal activity, and a greater appreciation of life (Robbins and Anthony, 1982). This is almost the opposite of what the media tells us about life in communes.

Children

Some controversy exists whether communal life is beneficial or detrimental to children. Authors such as Constantine and Constantine (1976), on group marriage, and Leslie and Karen Rabkin (1972), on kibbutzim, envision the communal setting as more or less a paradise for children:

> Contrary to alarmist predictions and not really surprisingly, the children growing up in these expanded families proved to be self-reliant but cooperative, competent more than competitive, friendly, robust and self-confident. They were happy with positive, realistic images of themselves. With few exceptions, children have fared uncommonly well in these families (Constantine and Constantine, 1977, p. 259-260).

> Meanwhile, we can sum up the Kibbutnik: he is a healthy, intelligent, generous, somewhat shy but warm human being, rooted in his community and the larger Israeli society (Rabkin and Rabkin, 1972, p. 99).

These views are perhaps too optimistic and only apply under ideal circumstances. Indeed, in stable communes where little turnover takes place, children can find more mutual support and security, be less isolated, develop a stronger sense of belonging, have more responsibility, have many adult role models, and learn from various older children of both sexes. As we have already seen, however, communes seldom survive more than a couple of years, and the turnover rate within enduring groups is high. When the group dissolves or members to whom the child was attached leave, the child can easily become insecure. Children are usually less able to cope with such radical transitions and losses. The battle of parental authority versus group authority in the upbringing of children can also serve to confuse the child. In only 33% of urban and 11% of rural communes, for instance, are the biological parents totally responsible for their children (Zablocki, 1980).

It is interesting to note here that the Israeli kibbutzim, which have managed to survive for several generations as a variant lifestyle, are now undergoing substantial changes, both with respect to gender-roles (as mentioned earlier) and the socialization of children — both in the direction of a more traditional pattern of everyday life. With respect to child-rearing, Israeli psychologists such as Amiram Raviv and Yair Palgi (1985) are finding that family units are becoming more important and that the biological parents are increasingly being delegated the role of main socializers. This is especially manifested in changing sleeping arrangements: whereas children used to sleep communally, a shift is presently taking place that promotes family-based sleeping arrangements.

Commitment

A main problem for many communal groups is the maintenance of commitment. Kanter (1972) notes that commitment to a communal group occurs at four different levels.

1) Organization. Commitment to the commune as an organization implies that one must be convinced that it is worthwhile to invest much effort and make various sacrifices that benefit the group as a whole. In successful communal groups, mechanisms are also usually found that reward behaviors that benefit the group.

2) Others. Commitment to other communards implies that these individuals become one's primary group, satisfying one's basic affective needs. The development of close interpersonal relations with other members is not always easy because it often entails the demand of loosening or even discontinuing bonds with other meaningful others, because commune members are still relative strangers, and because of the high turnover rates in communes. Mechanisms used to enhance commitment to others in the commune may include working together, sharing, steady group contacts and activities, joint responsibilities, endogamy (marriage strictly within the group), and group rituals.

3) Normative structure. The organization of everyday life is more complex in communes than in the previously discussed lifestyles, especially due to the simple fact that there are more individuals involved. Along with the ideological character of many communes, this leads to many explicit and elaborate behavioral codes.

4) Ideology. Committing oneself to the ideology of a group and its behavioral codes implies significant sacrifices on the part of the communard, especially with respect to personal autonomy. One of the primary mechanisms that communes use to facilitate commitment at this level is "mortification." In the mortification process, a person is told of all his/her weaknesses and shortcomings, and subsequently shown how adherence to the groups' behavioral codes is beneficial to that person. An emphasis on higher goals, which can only be reached by moral compliance and commitment, is also a phenomenon frequently encountered.

A high degree of commitment can hardly be expected in most communal arrangements, given the experimental function of the commune for many young adults, and considering the fact that individualistic values make people unwilling to sacrifice too much personal autonomy for the sake of group interests. Noreen Cornfield (1983, p. 124) cogently depicts the situation as follows: "In both historical utopias and contemporary communes, a norm of high involvement prolonged duration; but in the modern communes, this was true only when such involvement was not perceived as encroaching on the members' private time." In addition, members of many groups can easily enter and leave the commune, which again undermines commitment, a stable membership base, and a structured organization.

Stability

Given the foregoing, it should hardly be surprising that perhaps the most pronounced feature of communes is their instability, both in terms of membership turnover and the propensity to disintegrate. Studies of past and present communes constantly point to the ephemeral character of these groups. Though some, such as the Quakers, Shakers, the Amana Society, the Harmony Society, and the Hutterites survived for a century or more, the vast majority are so unstable that they soon perish. Kanter (1972) found that very few communes in past centuries were able to survive for more than a generation. In Zablocki's (1980) sample of 120 groups, the mean duration was a mere 2.4 years from the point he came into contact with them. Constantine and Constantine (1973) recorded the rapid dissolution of group marriages: 44% were still in existence after one year, 17% after three years, and 7% after five years. Given these poor success rates it is highly unlikely that an individual will spend a lifetime in one communal group.

In addition to lack of commitment, many other variables have been examined to account for the fact that some communes disband while others stay intact, including factors such as the organizational structure of the group, age distribution, ideological foundations, and arrangement of sexual activity. The following can be said about research in this area.

1) Degree of structuring. Explicit arrangements, behavioral codes, rules, regulations, and effective leadership, etc. are strongly related to survival chances (Kanter, 1972). Without structuring and leadership, disorganization becomes rampant, and conflicts emerge without the means of ameliorating the tensions that caused these conflicts. Jansen (1980), who researched communes in the Netherlands, divided his sample into groups with high, medium, or low degrees of structuring. Those with a high degree of structuring were three times as successful as those with a low degree, as measured after 2.5 years. A study of 92 communes by Jeni Mowery (1978) revealed similar patterns in the United States. Here, 93% of low-structured communes failed within 3 years time, while none lasted more than 15 years. For highly-structured communes these percentages were 32% and 36%, respectively.

2) Charismatic leadership. Strong leadership positively influences the survival rate of communes, especially when the charismatic leader is not in residence; members of groups with a charismatic leader in residence are more likely to be confronted with the leader's shortcomings (Zablocki, 1980).

3) Age. There is some evidence that groups with a higher mean membership age have a better change for survival. Zablocki (1980) found that members exhibit a significant decline in exiting behavior after 35 years of age. Jansen's (1980) study reveals that groups with a mean age of 26 or higher are six times more likely to survive for 2.5 years than groups with a mean age lower than 23.

4) Individualism. Communes emphasizing individualism tend to be less resilient to centrifugal forces than those emphasizing discipline. In Zablocki's (1980) subsample of psychological communes, for example, 89% had ceased to exist within four years, while for rehabilitational communes this was 25%.

5) Religion. Studies have consistently shown that religious groups have a better chance for survival than their secular counterparts (Kanter, 1972). Religion proves to be a binding force, especially if a religiously motivated group can survive the initial two years of existence (Zablocki, 1980).

6) Financial status. Communes that are financially well-off stand a better chance of succeeding. Mowery (1978) found that more than 80% of the groups with a "subsistence" level financial base survived less than 3 years. Only 2% lasted more than 15 years. Well-financed communes, on the other hand, had lower rates of dissolution. Of these, 32% folded within 3 years, but 36% managed to last 15 years or longer. Nevertheless, economic failure is seldom the primary reason given by communards for the disintegration of their commune (Zablocki, 1980).

7) Sex. The verdict is still out on whether *monogamy* or *non-exclusive sexuality* is more conducive to commune longevity. Most studies of contemporary communes show that nonexclusivity makes communal groups unstable because it creates fertile soil for intense conflict. For example, Zablocki (1980) found that of the communes in his sample which had disintegrated, 11% did so because of sexual issues. Other research has found that groups with multiple sexual relations between the members tend to be more stable than groups in which the members were monogamous (Van Ussel, 1977). Interestingly, however, two of the most successful communal movements of the past two centuries, the Shakers and the Harmonists, were celibate. By continually rejuvenating their ranks, the Shakers were able to survive for more than a century and a half.

REVIEW QUESTIONS

1) Do you consider the following arrangements to be communal and why? (a) Convents (b) Several roommates of the same sex sharing a house (c) Several roommates of both sexes sharing a house (d) A family sharing a house with aunts, uncles, and cousins (e) polygamous Mormon sectarian split-offs.
2) What is noteworthy about the characteristics of communards? How are these related to the motives for joining a commune?
3) How are commitment and communal success related?

SUGGESTED PROJECTS

1) Imagine someone asked you to construct a hypothetical model of a commune that would offer the best chances for success. With this chapter and your own ideas as a guide, try to construct such a model (think about things such as decision making, sexual relations, rules and regulations, division of labor, finances, etc.). Discuss this in class.

2) Ask two friends or relatives the following questions about communes:

   True or False?

   a. Living in communal groups is something that has only come into practice during the last few decades in the United States.

   b. Psychologically speaking, communards don't really differ all that much from their peers.

   c. Commune members tend to come from close-knit, intact families.

   d. After joining a commune the members tend to become more radical by engaging in activities such as using drugs and participating in political demonstrations.

   e. People who decide to live in communes are usually very irreligious.

   Discuss the responses to these questions in class.

3) Make a list of what you think the costs and benefits of communal life would be for you, both as a temporary and as a permanent lifestyle.

CHAPTER
7

Epilogue

IN THIS LAST CHAPTER, we would like to reflect upon, and summarize, some of the themes that have been presented in the foregoing chapters, particularly the reasons individuals become involved in variant lifestyles, including the role of personality factors, the issue of commitment, the crosscultural context of variant lifestyles and relationships, and the association of such lifestyles with the individualistic value pattern in American society.

INVOLVEMENT IN VARIANT LIFESTYLES

We have emphasized that very different factors and processes can move people into variant lifestyles and relationships. In some instances, ideologically based, conscious decisions to adapt a variant lifestyle occur, as is true for many sexually open marriages and communes as well as for those cohabitational unions that are based on a rejection of the marital institution. In other cases, a certain lifestyle is forced upon an individual, i.e., when people become or stay single because of factors outside of their own control, such as the death of a spouse or the shortage of available partners. Similarly, a sexual preference for members of one's own sex can leave an individual few options other than to become engaged in homosexual relationships, although, of course, the particular form of these relationships is, to a large extent, a matter of choice. But even when people seem to be able to freely choose their own lifestyle, in many cases no conscious decisions are apparent. For instance, in a gradual process of increasing involvement and intimacy, couples may drift into cohabitation without any explicit discussion. In a similar vein, getting involved in an extramarital affair is often a rather gradual process where the participants prepare themselves for the act of adultery. And staying permanently single after a divorce may sometimes happen more or less automatically — even when suitable partners are available.

The reasons why, and the processes through which, people become involved in variant lifestyles may be even more complex than we suggest. A noteworthy fact is that a number of lifestyles and relationships are associated with relatively low degrees of mental health and psychological well-being. Although some lifestyles seem to be more prevalent among the well-educated and affluent who have freed themselves from the constraints of traditional religion, some people involved in variant lifestyles seem to have problems coping with their lives and with establishing satisfying intimate relationships. Thus, as far as research *does* show differences it seems that the satisfaction and the love in cohabiting relationships are generally lower than in marriage, that the unmarried (particularly the divorced and those living alone) suffer more from loneliness and health problems, that extramarital relationships (particularly when not approved by the spouse) may stem from feelings of alienation and unhappiness, that swingers and couples with sexually open marriages have been in therapy significantly more often, and that divorced people, swingers, cohabitors, and never-marrieds often have unhappy childhoods and come from unhappy family backgrounds. While current low mental and physical health may be the consequence of being in a deviant lifestyle, and its concomitant societal discrimination, this can not, of course, be true for factors in the family backgrounds of those involved in a given lifestyle. In this context, it is interesting to examine individuals involved in a lifestyle that is looked upon more negatively by society than all other lifestyles dealt with in this book, i.e., homosexuality. Despite the relatively unstable relationships found among lesbians and gays, homosexuals do *not* show signs of maladjustment, which illustrates that it is rather unlikely that even severe discrimination, as such, leads to mental health problems.

A factor accounting for the low sense of well-being found in some variant lifestyles, particularly in some groups of singles, is the lack of partner support in the broadest sense of the word. Indeed, we have seen that as far as loneliness is concerned, it is not the existence of a legally sanctioned relationship that is the crucial factor, but the presence of an intimate partner with whom one shares a life and in whom one can confide. However, the acquisition of such a relationship is much harder for some individuals than for others in contemporary society. A certain personality make-up, a specific set of attitudes, expectations, behavioral tendencies, and emotional reactions concerning intimate relationships that have their roots in one's family and childhood may affect the development of a satisfying close relationship. For instance, in reviewing the effects of parental divorce on later intimate relationships, Shaver and Rubenstein (1980) concluded that living through the divorce of one's parents, especially when very young, seems to predispose a person to later loneliness, lower self-esteem, distrust of others, and, in general, pessimistic attitudes about oneself and others. Such factors may have detrimental effects on the ability to begin, build, and maintain intimate relationships. In addition, an insecure childhood environment may foster a strong need for dependency in an intimate relationship that, at the same time, is feared. This might either lead to being clingy, or being aloof and distant, but in both cases fear of rejection is predominant.

It should be emphasized that such attitudes do not develop in all adults with unhappy childhoods, and this pattern is not characteristic for most people involved in lifestyles such as singlehood or cohabitation. Even more so, especially for some single women, singlehood may be a choice reflecting independence and maturity, and be accompanied by satisfying relationships with peers. Nevertheless, it seems that the pattern we described as being related to unhappy childhood backgrounds may play a role among a sizable minority of those involved in variant lifestyles, i.e., those who have problems with intimacy and commitment, those who have been divorced repeatedly, or those who have moved from one cohabiting or extramarital relationship to another. Noteworthy exceptions to this pattern are many communards, who frequently come from happy, unbroken families — and it looks as if many of them are seeking at least a temporary substitute for the family of their childhood to help them to make the transition to adulthood. But here again, it seems that experiences with intimate relationships in childhood have an influence on attitudes and preferences in (young) adulthood.

COMMITMENT

It must be noted that the low degree of commitment characteristic of many relationships outside of marriage must not in itself be seen as a negative aspect. We have presented various conceptualizations of commitment, several of which are similar to concepts of cohesion and dependency, and focused on all the factors that keep a person in a relationship or lifestyle, including the rewards of it, the investments one has made in it, and the attractiveness of the available alternatives. However, in line with Harold Kelley (1983), we prefer to view commitment as *the degree of invariant support for a relationship or lifestyle over time,* in spite of frustrations, problems, and the availability of attractive alternative options. Simply stated, commitment is the intention to put effort into the lifestyle or relationship and to work things out when difficulties arise. Such a commitment should be seen as something that is functional in some, but not adequate in other, circumstances. Being committed to a relationship in which one is abused, mistreated, or severely limited in one's personal growth can be rather self-destructive. In addition, for many in certain periods of their life, when they are recuperating from a divorce or are finishing school for instance, being relatively uncommitted to another person may be the best thing to do since emotional energy can be devoted to other tasks in life. Furthermore, it seems evident that many people, e.g., those who are heavily involved in their work, those who have a strong need for autonomy and freedom, or those who simply prefer to be on their own, may not need a close committed relationship with another person, and may attach relatively little importance to developing such a relationship. Indeed, for their own well-being, as well as for the well-being of others, it might be rather functional if they avoid commitment and do not give in to social pressure to become deeply involved in an intimate relationship. But lack of commitment can be problematic when the person involved longs for a close, committed relationship, but anxieties, fears, and lack of relational competence become a barrier to attaining the desired state of intimacy, or when children are involved and one or both partners are scared of the responsibilities this entails and the commitment it requires.

CROSS-CULTURAL CONTEXT

It will have become apparent that criticism of marriage and all kinds of variant lifestyles is a recurrent and persistent historical phenomenon, and that marriage continues to be a popular institution in America, especially when compared with other Western countries. Throughout this book we have presented data on attitudes toward non-conventional lifestyles in the United States and Western Europe, particularly the Netherlands. In general, the Dutch are found to be more tolerant and accepting of non-traditional forms than the Americans. At this point, we would like to emphasize that the difference between these countries is not simply a matter of more or less permissiveness. There are also qualitative, often historically rooted differences, in the meaning of marriage and parenthood. Historically, marriage has been less popular in Western Europe than in the United States. Long after the Industrial Revolution, European marriage was based primarily on economic and rational grounds. The continuation of family property and the expected instrumental role fulfillment by the spouses were the main factors taken into consideration. The parents had, much more so than in North America, a final say in the decision of whom their children were to marry, and marriage was primarily a unit for production and reproduction. There was often little affection between the spouses. Furthermore, extended families were quite common, and marital and family life was often controlled to a great extent by the larger community.

In contrast, in the United States the nuclear family as a separate unit was probably the prevailing residential unit long before the Industrial Revolution. Families were spatially and socially more isolated from the surrounding community, the influence of the parents on the courtship process was less, and the houses were larger, facilitating private sexual relations. Because of the large amount of land available, economic considerations played a less important role in the choice of a mate. Indeed, in contrast to the Netherlands, male-female relationships in the United States seem to have been remarkably egalitarian and lacking extended family controls as far back as the beginning of the nineteenth century. It therefore seems that the notion of marriage, based on the mutual love between husband and wife, was characteristic of American marriage long before it became the predominant concept of marriage in Western Europe (Buunk, 1983; Shorter, 1975; Pickett, 1978; Reiss, 1980).

However, despite a less positive attitude toward marriage, this institution has long been much more stable in the Netherlands than in the United States. With the exception of the temporary post World War II increase, the Dutch family has always been characterized by a low divorce rate in comparison not only with the United States, but also with most other Western European countries such as Denmark, Sweden, Austria, and France. In general, divorce is much more prevalent in the United States than in Western Europe. It is as though Western Europeans have more of a matter-of-fact attitude toward marriage. Thus, people in the Netherlands seem less inclined to marry for romantic reasons, few object to premarital sex and cohabitation and, once people are married, they are not as likely to consider extramarital sex as a serious breach of loyalty, one leading to divorce. Interestingly, however, unwed parenthood is much less prevalent in the Netherlands, partially because the easy acceptance of premarital sex has made contraceptives widely available. At the same time, there is a stronger adherence to an equal division of child care and household responsibilities. But, strangely enough, there is still a relatively low percentage of gainfully employed wives (Buunk, 1983).

VARIANT LIFESTYLES AND AMERICAN SOCIETY

Although it has been argued that there will be a swing back to traditional values in Western societies and, therefore, to increased disapproval of variant lifestyles partially as a result of the pressure of conservative religious groups, this seems rather unlikely in the long run. Of course, the current AIDS crisis has had a negative effect upon attitudes towards homosexuality and sexually open arrangements. But Western countries are, in a fundamental way, characterized by an individualistic value pattern, in which a high value is placed on the possibility to follow one's own desires and needs instead of subsuming one's interests to those of kin, community, or family. The values regarding the relationship between the individual and the collectivity constitute one of the central dimensions along which cultures differ. In some cultures, individualism is seen as a blessing and a source of well-being. Everyone is supposed to take care of him or herself, an individual identity is highly valued, and everyone has a right to a private life and a right to follow one's own desires and needs. Historically, for marital relationships, an individualistic value pattern coincided with the freedom of marital choice. Today one of the consequences of this value pattern is that individual interests are given priority over those of the relationship. A recent study by Bram Buunk and Ralph Hupka (1986) in seven nations showed that an emphasis upon following one's own independent interests in intimate relationships was much more prevalent in affluent, democratic countries such as the United States and the Netherlands than in relatively poor and nondemocratic nations such as the Soviet Union and Yugoslavia. Given the individualistic value pattern, it seems likely that the option to choose various lifestyles and relationships without being subjected to social disapproval is more central to the American value pattern than is sometimes supposed.

Indeed, many lifestyles discussed in this book have developed into an intrinsic part of the American way of intimate life. For example, half of the marriages will end in divorce and about a similar percentage of marriages will be affected by extramarital relationships. Also, during a substantial part of their lives, particularly while in their twenties, most adults remain unmarried and an increasing number of individuals cohabit before getting married. Although a long-term marriage continues to be the cultural ideal, and the chances for a satisfying, intimate, and equal relationship may be better than ever before in human history, at the same time the emphasis upon self-fulfillment in our culture and the decreased stigmatization of nonmarital options make marriages more vulnerable and less stable than in the past.

What does the future hold in store for us? Although future changes in marital and family life may be complex and varied we feel that variant lifestyles and relationships are definitely here to stay, but it is unlikely that they will become much more prevalent in the near future than they are now. Communal groups will always be around, serving the needs of selected groups (Settler, 1987), although these groups will continue to constitute only tiny minorities within the total population. Singlehood will remain a more or less voluntary stage in the life of most adults, but it is unlikely that the percentage of those who opt for lifelong singlehood will increase significantly. A steady percentage of the population in our society will always be exclusively homosexual. Extramarital relationships will affect many marriages, but when we take into account that the incidence of such relationships has hardly increased since the Kinsey studies conducted in the thirties and forties, it is unrealistic to expect a sharp rise in the prevalence of extramarital sex in the near future. As we have indicated several times, the deadly disease AIDS is having a tremendous impact upon the willingness to engage in sexually open lifestyles, and there are clear indications that there is currently a shift away from uncommitted, casual sex. But even after a cure for AIDS is found, it seems unlikely that sexually open marriages, group marriages, and similar arrangements have much chance of ever attracting substantial minorities within the American population, given the negative attitudes toward these behaviors and all the emotional and practical problems they seem to entail. Cohabitation, in contrast, seems to have become a modern courtship institution. However, the emotional significance of marriage in America, where it is viewed as a step indicating commitment, makes it unlikely that living together will become a substitute for marriage for most Americans in the near future.

References

Abbott, S., & Love, B. (1978). *Sappho was a right-on woman: A liberated view of lesbianism.* New York: Stein & Day.

Adams, M. (1976). *Single blessedness.* New York: Basic Books.

Aidala, A. A. (1984). Worldviews, ideologies and social experimentation: Clarification and replication of "The consciousness reformation." *Journal for the Scientific Study of Religion 23*(1), 44-59.

Alwin, D. F., Converse, P. E., & Martin, S. F. (1985). Living arrangements and social integration. *Journal of Marriage and the Family 47*(2), 319-334.

Anderson, D., & Braito, R. (1981). The mental health of the never married. *Alternative Lifestyles 4,* 108-124.

Argyle, M., & Henderson, M. (1985). *The anatomy of relationships.* Harmondsworth: Penguin Books.

Athanasiou, R., Shaver, P., & Tarvis, C. (1970). Sex. *Psychology Today 4,* 39-52.

Atwater, L. (1979). Getting involved: Women's transition to first extramarital sex. *Alternative Lifestyles 2,* 33-68.

Atwater, L. (1982). *The extramarital connection.* New York: Irvington.

Austrom, D., & Hanel, N. (1985). Psychological issues of single life in Canada: An exploratory study. *International Journal of Women's Studies 8,* 12-23.

Barkas, J. (1980). *Single in America.* New York: Atheneum.

Bartell, G. D. (1971). *Group sex.* New York: Wyden.

Batchelor, W. F. (1984). AIDS. *American Psychologist 39* (11), 1277-1278.

Bell, R. R. (1971). *Social deviance.* Homewood, Ill.: Dorsey Press.

Bell, R. R., & Peltz, D. (1974). Extramarital sex among women. *Medical Aspects of Human Sexuality 8,* 10-31.

Bell, R. R., Turner, S., & Rosen, L. (1975). A multi-variate analysis of female extramarital coïtus. *Journal of Marriage and the Family 37,* 375-383.

Bellah, R. (1976). The new religious consciousness and the crisis in modernity. In C. Glock & R. Bellah (Eds.), *The new religious consciousness,* (pp. 333-352). Berkeley, CA: University of California Press.

Ben-Rafael, E., & Weitman, S. (1984). The reconstruction of the family in the Kibbutz. Archives Europeencs de Sociologie 25, 1-27.

Bennett, J. (1975). Communes and communitarianism. *Theory and Society 2,* 63-94.

Berger, B. M. (1988, Jan./Feb.). Utopia and its environment. *Society*: 37-41.

Berger, B. M., Hackett, B., & Miller, R. M. (1972). Supporting the communal family. In Rosabeth M. Kanter (Ed.) *Communes: Creating and managing the collective life.* (p. 253) New York: Harper & Row.

Bernard, J. (1973). *The future of marriage.* New York: Bantam.

Birdwhistell, R. L. (1970). The idealized model of the American family. *Social Casework 50,* 195-198.

Blasband, D., & Peplau, L. A. (1985). Sexual exclusivity versus openness in gay male couples. *Archives of Sexual Behavior 14*(5), 395-412.

Bloom, B., Asher, S., & White, S. (1978). Marital disruption as a stressor. *Psychological Bulletin 85*, 867-894.

Blumstein, P., & Schwartz, P. (1983). *American couples*. New York: William Morrow.

Bower, D. W., & Christopherson, V. A. (1977). University student cohabitation: A regional comparison of selected attitudes and behavior. *Journal of Marriage and the Family 39*(3), 447-453.

Brown, G. (1980). *The new celibacy*. New York: Ballantine Books.

Brubaker, T. H. (1985). *Later life families*. Beverly Hills, CA: Sage.

Burns, A. (1984). Perceived causes of marriage breakdown and conditions of life. *Journal of Marriage and the Family 46*, 551-562.

Buunk, B. (1980a). Extramarital sex in the Netherlands. Motivations in social and marital context. *Alternative Lifestyles 3*, 11-39.

Buunk, B. (1980b). Sexually open marriages. Ground rules for countering potential threats to marriage. *Alternative Lifestyles, 3*, 312-328.

Buunk, B. (1981). Jealousy in sexually open marriages. *Alternative Lifestyles 4*, 357-372.

Buunk, B. (1982a). Strategies of jealousy: Styles of coping with extramarital relationships of the spouse. *Family Relations 31*, 9-14.

Buunk, B. (1982b). Anticipated sexual jealousy: Its relationship to self-esteem, dependency and reciprocity. *Personality and Social Psychology Bulletin 8*, 310-316(b).

Buunk, B. (1983). Alternative lifestyles in international perspective. A transatlantic comparison. In E. D. Mackin & R. H. Rubin (Eds.), *Contemporary families and alternative lifestyles*. Beverly Hills, CA: Sage.

Buunk, B. (1984). Jealousy as related to attributions for the partner's behavior. *Social Psychology Quarterly 47*(1), 107-112.

Buunk, B. (1986). Husbands' jealousy. In R. A. Lewis & R. E. Salt (Eds.), *Men in families*. Beverly Hills, CA: Sage.

Buunk, B. (1987a). Conditions that promote breakups as a consequence of extradyadic involvements. *Journal of Social and Clinical Psychology 5*(2), 237-250.

Buunk, B. (1987b) Long-term stability and change in sexually open marriages. In L. Shamgar-Handelman & R. Palomba (Eds.), *Alternative patterns of family life in modern societies*. Rome: Instituto di Richerche sulla Popolazione (Collana Monografie 1).

Buunk, B., & Hupka, R. B. (1986). Autonomy in close relationships: A cross-cultural study. *Family Perspective 20*(3), 209-221.

Buunk, B., & Bringle, R. G. (1987). Jealousy in love relationships. In D. Perlman & S. Duck (Eds.), *Intimate relationships: Development, dynamics and deterioration*. Newbury Park, CA: Sage.

Caldwell, M. A., & Peplau, L. A. (1984). The balance of power in lesbian relationships. *Sex Roles 10* (7/8), 587-599.

Caplow, T., Bahr, H. M., Chadwick, B. A., Hill, R., & Holmes Williamson, M. (1982). *Middletown Families. Fifty years of change and continuity*. Minneapolis: University of Minnesota Press.

Cargan, L. (1986). Stereotypes of singles: A cross-cultural comparison. *International Journal of Comparative Sociology 27*, 200-208.

Cargan, L., & Melko, M. (1982). *Singles. Myths and realities,* Beverly Hills, CA: Sage.

Carrol, L. (1988). Concern with AIDS and the sexual behavior of college students. *Journal of Marriage and Family 50*, 405-411.

Cass, V. C. (1984). Homosexual identity formation: Testing a theoretical model. *Journal of Sex Research 20*(2), 143-167.

Cazenave, N. A. (1980). Alternate intimacy, marriage, and family lifestyles among low-income Black-Americans. *Alternative Lifestyles 4*(4), 425-444.

Chapman, B. E., & Brannock, J. C. (1987). Proposed model of lesbian identity develo ment: An empirical examination. *Journal of Homosexuality 14*(3/4), 69-80.

Cherlin, A. J. (1981). *Marriage, divorce, remarriage.* Cambridge, MA: Harvard University Press.

Christensen H. T. (1973). "Attitudes toward marital infidelity: a nine-culture sampling of university student opinion." Journal of Comparative Family Studies 4, 197-214.

Clayton, R. R., & Voss, H. L. (1977). Shacking up: Cohabitation in the 1970's. *Journal of Marriage and the Family 39*(2), 273-283.

Cogswell, B. E. (1975). Variant family forms and lifestyles: Rejection of the traditional nuclear family. *Family Coordinator 24*(4), 391-406.

Cole, C. L. (1977). Cohabitation in social context. In R. W. Libby & R. N. Whitehurst (Eds.), *Marriage and alternatives: Exploring intimate relationships.* Glenview, IL: Scott, Foresman.

Cole, W. G. (1969). Religious attitudes towards extramarital intercourse. In G. Neubeck (Ed.), *Extramarital relations.* Englewood Cliffs, NJ: Prentice-Hall.

Conover, P. W. (1975). An analysis of communes and intentional communities with particular attention to sexual and gender relations. *Family Coordinator 24,* 453-464.

Conrad, P., & Schneider, J. W. (1980). *Deviance and medicalization: From badness to sickness.* St. Louis: CV Mosby Company.

Constantine, L., & Constantine, J. M. (1973). *Group marriage.* New York: Collier Books.

Constantine, L., & Constantine, J. M. (1976). *Treasures of the island: Children in alternative families.* Beverly Hills, CA: Sage Publications.

Constantine, L. J. (1985). Editor's note. *Lifestyles: A Journal of Changing Patterns 8*(1), 3-4.

Cornfield, N. (1983). The success of urban communes. *Journal of Marriage and the Family 48,* 115-126.

Cuber, J. F. (1969). Adultery: Reality versus stereotype. In G. Neubeck (Ed.), *Extramarital relations.* Englewood Cliffs, NJ: Prentice-Hall.

Cunningham, J. D., & Antill, J. K. (1981). Love in developing romantic relationships. In S. Duck & R. Gilmour (Eds.), *Personal relationships 2: Developing personal relationships.* London: Academic Press.

Darling, J. (1981). Late marrying bachelors. In P. J. Stein (Ed.), *Single life: Unmarried adults in social context.* New York: St. Martin's.

De Groot, B., & Visser, F. (1984). *Homosexuality in the Netherlands* (In Dutch). Unpublished paper.

De Jong-Gierveld, J. (1980). Singlehood: A creative or a lonely experience? *Alternative Lifestyles 3,* 350-368.

De Jong-Gierveld, J. (1986). *The (marital) partner as a source of social support in everyday and problem situations.* Paper presented at the 3rd International Conference on Personal Relationships. Hezlya, Israel, July.

De Maris, A., & Leslie, G. R. (1984). Cohabitation with the future spouse: Its influence upon marital satisfaction and communication. *Journal of Marriage and the Family 46*(1), 77-84.

De Monteflores, C., & Schultz, S. J. (1978). Coming out: Similarities and differences for lesbians and gay men. *Journal of Social Issues 34*(3), 59-72.

Denfield, D. (1974). Dropouts from swinging: The marriage counselor as informant. In J. R. Smith, & L. G. Smith (Eds.), *Beyond monogamy. Recent studies of sexual alternatives in marriage.* Baltimore and London: Johns Hopkins University Press.

Denfield, D., & Gordon, M. (1970). The sociology of mate swapping: Or the family that swings together clings together. *Journal of Sex Research 6*, 85-100.

Doudna, C., & McBride, F. (1981). Where are the men for the women at the top? In P. J. Stein (Ed.), *Single life: Unmarried adults in social context.* New York: St. Martin's.

Duckworth, J., & Levitt, E. I. (1985). Personality analysis of a swingers' club. *Lifestyles: A Journal of Changing Patterns 8*(1), 35-45.

Edwards, M., & Stinnett, N. (1974). Perceptions of college students concerning alternate life styles. *The Journal of Psychology 87*, 143-156.

Ellis, L., & Ames, A. (1987). Neurohormonal functioning and sexual orientation. *Psychological Bulletin, 101*(2), 233-258.

Erickson, J. A. (1980). Race, sex, and alternate lifestyle choices. *Alternative Lifestyles 3*(4), 405-424.

Erikson, E. (1963). *Youth: Change and challenge.* New York: Basic Books.

Etzkowitz, H., & Stein, P. (1978). The life spiral: Human needs and adult roles. *Alternative Lifestyles 1*(4), 434-446.

Faderman, L. (1984). The 'New Gay' lesbians. *Journal of Homosexuality 10*(3/4), 85-95.

Fairfield, R. (1972). *Communes. U.S.A.* Baltimore: Penguin.

Fang, B. (1976). Swinging: In retrospect. *Journal of Sex Research 12*(3), 220-237.

Ford, C. S., & Beach, F. A. (1952). *Patterns of sexual behavior.* New York: Harper.

Gagnon, J., & Simon, W. (1973). *Sexual conduct: The social sources of human sexuality.* Chicago: Aldine.

Gallup Report (1987). *Report Nos.* 244-245, 2-9.

Gerstel, N. R. (1969). Marital alternatives and the regulation of sex: Commuter couples as a test case. *Alternative Lifestyles 2*, 145-176.

Gilmartin, B. G. (1974). Sexual deviance and social networks. A study of social, family and marital interaction patterns among co-marital sex participants. In J. R. Smith & L. G. Smith (Eds.), *Beyond monogamy. Recent studies of sexual alternatives in marriage.* Baltimore and London: Johns Hopkins University Press.

Gilmartin, B. G. (1977). Jealousy among the swingers. In G. Clanton & L. G. Smith (Eds.), *Jealousy.* Englewood Cliffs, NJ: Prentice-Hall.

Glass, G. P., & Wright, T. L. (1977). The relationship of extramarital sex, length of marriage, and sex difference on marital satisfaction and romanticism: Athanasiou's data reanalyzed. *Journal of Marriage and the Family 39*, 691-704.

Glass, G. P., & Wright, T. L. (1985). Sex difference in type of extramarital involvement and marital dissatisfaction. *Sex Roles 12*, 1101-1120.

Glenn, N. D., & Weaver, C. N. (1979). Attitudes toward premarital, extramarital and homosexual relations in the U.S. in the 1970's. *Journal of Sex Research 15*, 108-118.

Glick & Norton, (1977).

Gove, W. R. (1972a). The relationship between sex roles, marital status, and mental illness. *Social Forces 51*, 34-44.

Gove, W. R. (1972b). Sex, marital status and suicide. *Journal of Health and Social Behavior 13*, 204-213.

Gove, W. R. (1974). Sex, marital status, and mortality. *American Journal of Sociology 79*(1), 45-66.

Green, R. (1977). *The "sissy boy syndrome" and the development of homosexuality.* New Haven, CT: Yale University Press.

Green, R., Mandel, J. B., Hotvedt, M. E., Gray, J., & Smith, L. (1986). Lesbian mothers and their children: A comparison with solo parent heterosexual mothers and their children. *Archives of Sexual Behavior 15*(2)

Gwartney-Gibbs, P. A. (1986). The institutionalization of premarital cohabitation: Estimates from marriage license applications. *Journal of Marriage and the Family 48*, 423-434.

Hanna, S. L., & Knaub, P. K. (1981). Cohabitation before remarriage: Its relationship to family strengths. *Alternative Lifestyles 4*(4), 507-522.

Harris, L., & Westin, A. F. (1979). *The dimensions of privacy: A national opinion research survey of attitudes toward privacy.* Stevens Point, WI: Sentry Insurance.

Harry, J. (1983). Gay male and lesbian relationships. In E. D. Macklin & R. H. Rubin (Eds.), *Contemporary families and alternative fifestyles.* Beverly Hills, CA: Sage.

Hansson, R. O., Jones, W. H., & Carpenter, B. N. (1984). Relational competence and social support. *Review of Personality and Social Psychology 5*, 265-284.

Higginbotham, E. (1981). Is marriage a priority? In P. J. Stein (Ed.), *Single life: Unmarried adults in social context.* New York: St. Martin's.

Hitchens, D. (1980). Social attitudes, legal standards, and personal trauma in child custody cases. *Journal of Homosexuality 5*, 89-95.

Houseknecht, S. K., Vaughan, S., & Statham, A. (1987). The impact of singlehood on the career patterns of professional women. *Journal of Marriage and the Family 49*(2), 333-366.

Humphreys, L. (1970). *Tearoom trade.* Chicago: Aldine.

Hunt, N. (1974). *Sexual behavior in the 1970s.* Chicago: Dell Publishing Co.

Jaffe, D. T., & Kanter, R. M. (1976). Couple strains in communal households: A four-factor model of the separation process. *Journal of Social Issues 32*(1), 169-191.

Jansen, H. A. M. (1980). Communes. *Alternative Lifestyles 3*, 255-277.

Jenks, R. J. (1985a). A comparative study of swingers and non-swingers: Attitudes and beliefs. *Lifestyles: A Journal of Changing Patterns 8*(1), 5-20.

Jenks, R. J. (1985b). Swinging: A test of two theories and a proposed new model. *Archives of Sexual Behavior 14*, 517-525.

Kanter, R. M. (1972). *Commitment and community: Communes and utopias in sociological perspective.* Cambridge, MA: Harvard University Press.

Kelley, H. H. (1983). Love and commitment. In H. H. Kelley, E. Berscheid, A. Christensen, J. H. Harvey, T. L. Huston, S. Levinger, E. McClintock, L. A. Replan, & D. R. Peterson. *Close relationships.* New York: W. H. Freeman.

Keniston, K. (1960). *The uncommitted: Alienated youth in American Society.* New York: Dell.

Kinsey, A., Pomeroy, W., & Gebhard, P. H., Martin, C. E. (1953). *Sexual behavior in the human female.* Philadelphia: W. B. Saunders.

Kinsey, A., Pomeroy, W., & Martin, C. (1948). *Sexual behavior in the human male.* Philadelphia: W. B. Saunders.

Kirkham, G. L. (1971). Homosexuality in prison. In J. M. Henslin (Ed.), *Studies in the sociology of sex.* New York: Appleton-Century-Crofts.

Knapp, J. (1976). An exploratory study of seventeen sexually open marriages. *Journal of Sex Research 12*, 206-219.

Knapp, J. J., & Whitehurst, R. N. (1977). Sexually open marriage and relationships: Issues and prospects. In R. W. Libby & R. N. Whitehurst (Eds.), *Marriage and alternatives: Exploring intimate relationships.* Glenview, IL: Scott, Foresman and Company.

Kotkin, M. (1985). To marry or to live together? *Lifestyles: A Journal of Changing Patterns* 7(3), 156-170.

Kottack, C. P. (1974). *Anthropology: Exploration of human diversity.* New York: Random House.

Kurdeck, L. A., & Schmitt, J. P. (1986). Relationship quality of partners in heterosexual, married, heterosexual cohabiting, and gay and lesbian relationships. *Journal of Personality and Social Psychology* 51(4), 711-720.

Kurdeck, L. A., & Schmitt, J. P. (1987). Perceived emotional support from family and friends in members of homosexual, married and heterosexual cohabiting couples. *Journal of Homosexuality* 14(3/4), 57-67.

Le Roy Ladurie, E. (1974), *Montaillou.* Harmondsworth: Penguin Books.

Levine, S. V. (1984). Radical departures. *Psychology Today 8,* 20-27.

Lewis, R. A., Spanier, G. B., Atkinson, V. L., & Lettecka, C. F. (1977). Commitment in married and unmarried cohabitation. *Social Focus 10,* 367-374.

Libby, R. W. (1977). Creative singlehood as a sexual lifestyle: Beyond marriage as a rite of passage. In R. W. Libby & R. N. Whitehurst (Eds.), *Marriage and alternatives: Exploring intimate relationships.* Glenview, IL: Scott, Foresman and Company.

Libby, R. W., & Whitehurst, R. N. (Eds.). (1973). *Renovating marriage.* Danville, CA: Consensus Publishers.

Lofland, J., & Stark, R. (1965). Becoming a world-saver. *American Sociological Review 30,* 862-879.

Lynch, J. M., & Reilly, M. E. (1985/1986). Role relationships: Lesbian perspectives. *Journal of Homosexuality* 12(2), 53-69.

Macklin, E. D. (1974). Students who live together: Trial marriage or going very steady? *Psychology Today 11,* 53-59.

Macklin, E. D. (1980). Nontraditional family forms: A decade of research. *Journal of Marriage and the Family* 42(4), 905-922.

Macklin, E. D. (1983). Nonmarital heterosexual cohabitation: An overview. In E. D. Macklin & R. H. Rubin (Eds.), *Contemporary Families and Alternative Lifestyles.* Beverly Hills, CA: Sage.

Macklin, E. D. (1987). Nontraditional family forms. In M. B. Sussmann & S. K. Steinmetz (Eds.), *Handbook of marriage and the family.* New York: Plenum Press.

Marciano, T. D. (1975). Variant family forms in a world perspective. *Family Coordinator* 24(4), 407-420.

Maslow, A. (1970). *Motivation and personality.* New York: Harper & Row.

McClosky, H. B., & Brill, A. (1983). *Dimensions of tolerance: What Americans believe about civil liberties.* New York: Russell Sage.

McWhirter, D. P., & Mattison, A. M. (1984). *The male couple: How relationships develop.* Englewood Cliffs, NJ: Prentice-Hall.

Meyering, R. A., & Epling-McWerther, E. A. (1986). Decision-making in extramarital relationships. *Lifestyles, A Journal of Changing Patterns* 8:(2), 115-129.

Middendorp, C. P. (1975). Further cultural developments in the Netherlands? The period 1970-1974 (In Dutch). *Intermediair* 11(19), 1-5.

Mika, K., & Bloom, B. (1980). Adjustment to separation among former cohabitors. *Journal of Divorce 4,* 45-66.

Minton, H. L., & McDonald, G. J. (1983/1984). Homosexual identity formation as a developmental process. *Journal of Homosexuality* 9(2/3), 91-104.

Minturn, L. (1984). Sex-role differentiation in contemporary communes. *Sex Roles* 10(1/2), 73-85.

Morin, S. F., Charles, K. A., & Malyon, A. K. (1984). The psychological impact of AIDS on gay men. *American Psychologist 39*(11), 1288-1293.

Mowery, J. (1978). Systemic requisites of communal groups. *Alternative Lifestyles 1*(2), 235-261.

Muncy, R. L. (1988 Jan./Feb.). Sex and marriage in Utopia. *Society:* 46-48.

Murstein, B. I. (1974). *Love, sex and marriage through the ages.* New York: Springer.

Murstein, B. I. (1978). Swinging or comarital sex. In B. I. Murstein (Ed.), *Exploring intimate lifestyles.* New York: Springer.

Murstein, B. I., Chalpin, M. J., Heard, K. V., & Vyse, S. A. (1989). Sexual behavior, drugs and relationship patterns on a college campus over thirteen years. *Adolescence* (in press).

Neubeck, G. (1969). *Extramarital relations.* Englewood Cliffs, NJ: Prentice-Hall.

Newcomb, M. D. (1981). Heterosexual cohabitation relationships. In S. Duck & R. Gilmour (Eds.), *Personal relationships Vol. 1.* London: Academic Press.

Newcomb, M. D. (1983). Relationship qualities of those who live together. *Alternative Lifestyles 6,* 78-102.

Newcomb, M. D. (1986a). Cohabitation, marriage and divorce among adolescents and young adults. *Journal of Social and Personal Relationships 3,* 473-494.

Newcomb, M. D. (1986b). Sexual behavior of cohabitors: A comparison of three independent samples. *The Journal of Sex Research 22*(4), 492-513.

O'Neill, N., & O'Neill, G. (1972). Open marriage: A synergic model. *Family Coordinator 21*(4), 403-409.

Oudijk, C. (1983). *Social atlas of women* (In Dutch). Den Haag, The Netherlands: Staats Uitgeverij.

Parmelee, P. A., & Werner, C. (1978). Stereotypes of lonely city dwellers. *Personality and Social Psychology Bulletin* 292-295.

Peplau, L. A., & Amaro, H. (1982). Understanding lesbian relationships. In J. Weinreich & W. Paul (Eds.), *Homosexuality: Social, psychological and biological issues.* Beverly Hills, CA: Sage.

Peplau, L. A., & Cochran, S. D. (1987). A relationship perspective on homosexuality. In D. P. McWhirter, S. A. Sanders, & J. M. Reinisch (Eds.), *Homosexuality/heterosexuality: The Kinsey scale and current research.* New York: Oxford University Press.

Peplau, L. A., Cochran, S., & Rook, K. (1978). Loving women: Attachment and autonomy in lesbian relationships. *Journal of Social Issues 34*(3), 7-27.

Peplau, L. A., & Gordon, S. L. (1983). The intimate relations of lesbians and gay men. In E. R. Allgeier & N. B. McCormick (Eds.), *Changing boundaries: Gender roles and sexual behavior.* Palo Alto, CA: Mayfield.

Peplau, L. A., & Perlman, D. (Eds.). 1982. *Loneliness: A source book of current theory, research and therapy.* New York: Wiley.

Perrucci, C. C., & Targ, D. B. (Eds.). (1974). *Marriage and the family: A critical analysis and proposals for change.* New York: David McKay.

Pickett, R. S. (1978). Monogamy on trial. Part II, the modern era. *Alternative Lifestyles 1,* 281-302.

Pietropinto, A., & Simenauer, J. (1977). *Beyond the male myth: What women want to know about men's sexuality. A nationwide survey.* New York: Times Book.

Plummer, K. (1981). Building a sociology of homosexuality. In K. Plummer (Ed.), *The making of the modern homosexual* (pp. 17-29). London: Hutchinson.

Queen, C. (1987). The politics of AIDS: A review essay. *The Insurgent Sociologist 14*(2), 103-124.

Rabkin, L., & Rabkin, K. (1972). Children of the Kibbutz. In M. Gordon (Ed.), *The Nuclear family in crisis: The search for an alternative.* (pp. 93-100). New York: Harper & Row.

Ramey, J. W. (1975). Intimate groups and networks: Frequent consequence of sexually open marriage. *Family Coordinator 24,* 515-530.

Rank, M. R. (1981). The transition to marriage: A comparison of cohabiting and dating relationships ending in marriage or divorce. *Alternative Lifestyles 4*(4), 487-506.

Rao, V. V. P., & Rao, V. N. (1980). Alternatives in intimacy, marriage and family lifestyles: Preferences of black college students. *Alternative Lifestyles 3*(4), 485-498.

Raviv, A., & Palgi, Y. (1985). The perception of social-environmental characteristics in Kibbutz families with family-based and communal sleeping arrangements. *Journal of Personality and Social Psychology 49*(2), 376-385.

Reinharz, S. (1988 Jan./Feb.). Creating Utopia for the elderly. *Society:* 52-58.

Reiss, I. (1980). *Family systems in America.* New York: Holt, Rinehart and Winston.

Reiss, I., Anderson, G. E., & Sponaugle, G. C. (1980). A multivariate model of the determinants of extramarital sexual permissiveness. *Journal of Marriage and the Family 52,* 395-411.

Reiss, I. (1986). A sociological journey into sexuality. *Journal of Marriage and the Family 48*(2), 233-242.

Richardson, J. (1983).

Richardson, J. T. (1978). Conversion careers. *Society* (March-April) 47-50.

Richardson, J. T. (1983). New religious movements in the United States. *Social Compass, 30*(1), 85-135.

Richardson, J. T. (1985). Psychological and psychiatric studies of new religions. In L. Brown (Ed.), *New perspectives in the psychology of religion.* Oxford: Pergamon Press.

Richardson, J. T. (1986). *AIDS: Social and legal implications.* Paper presented of the annual meeting of the Western Social Science Association. Reno, Nevada.

Richardson, J. T., Stewart, M., & Simmonds, R. (1978). *Organized miracles: A study of a contemporary, youth, communal, fundamentalist organization.* New Brunswick, NJ: Transaction Books.

Richardson, J. T., & van Driel, B. (1984). Public support for anti-cult legislation. *Journal for the Scientific Study of Religion 23*(4), 412-418.

Richardson, L. (1985). *The new other woman.* New York: The Free Press.

Richardson, L. (1986). Another world. *Anthropology & Education Quarterly, 20*(2), 22-27.

Ridley, C. A., Peterman, D. J., & Avery, A. W. (1978). Cohabitation: Does it make for a better marriage? *Family Coordinator 27*(2), 129-136.

Risman, B. J., Hill, C. T., Rubin, Z., & Peplau, L. A. (1981). Living together in college: Implications for courtship. *Journal of Marriage and the Family 43*(1), 77-83.

Robbins, T., & Anthony, D. (1982). Deprogramming, brainwashing and the medicalization of deviant religious groups. *Social Problems 29,* 283-297.

Rook, K. S.1984. Research on social support, loneliness and social isolation: Toward an integration. *Review of Personality and Social Psychology 5,* 239-264.

Roy,R., & Roy, D. (1973). Is monogamy outdated? In R. W. Libby & R. N. Whitehurst (Eds.), *Renovating marriage.* Danville, CA: Consensus Publishers.

Rubin, A. M. (1983). Open versus sexually exclusive marriage: A comparison of dyadic adjustment. *Alternative Lifestyles 5,* 101-109.

Rubin, A. M., & Adams, J. R. (1986). Outcomes of sexually open marriages. *Journal of Sex Research 22*, 311-319.

Safilios-Rothschild, C. (1969). Attitudes of Greek spouses toward marital infidelity. In G. Neubeck (Ed.), *Extramarital relations*. Englewood Cliffs, NJ: Prentice-Hall.

Saghir, M., & Robins, E. (1973). *Male and female homosexuality*. Baltimore: Williams & Williams.

Sanders, G. (1977). *The common and special aspects of the homosexual lifestyle* (In Dutch). Deventer: Van Loghum Slaterus.

Sauer, R. J. (1981). The live in boyfriend: A family arrangement. *Family Therapy 8*(3), 203-210.

Schelvis, N. (1983). Sex outside marriage (In Dutch). In *Sex in Nederland*. Utrecht: Het Spectrum.

Schur, E. M. (1965). *Crimes without victims*. Englewood Cliffs, NJ: Prentice-Hall.

Settler, B. H. (1987). A perspective on tomorrow's families. In M. B. Sussmann & S. K. Steinmetz (Eds.), *Handbook of marriage and the family*. New York: Plenum Press.

Shaver, P., & Rubenstein, C. (1980). Childhood attachment experience and adult loneliness. *Review of Personality and Social Psychology 1*, 42-73.

She, (1986). "The Devlin report," (pp. 108-113).

Shey, T. H. (1977). Why communes fail: A comparative analysis of the viability of Danish and American communes. *Journal of Marriage and the Family 39*, 605-613.

Shorter, E. (1975). *The making of the modern family*. New York: Basic Books.

Shostak, A. B. (1987). Singlehood. In M. B. Sussmann & S. K. Steinmetz (Eds.), *Handbook of marriage and the family*. New York: Plenum Press.

Shupe, A. D., & Bromley, D. G. (1980). *The new vigilantes*. Beverly Hills, CA: Sage.

Simenauer, J., & Carroll, D. (1982). *Singles. The new Americans*. New York: Signet.

Singh, B. K., Walton, B. L., & Williams, J. S. (1976). Extramarital sexual permissiveness: Conditions and contingencies. *Journal of Marriage and the Family 38*, 701-712.

Smith, J. R., & Smith, L. S. (Eds.) 1974. *Beyond monogamy. Recent studies of sexual alternatives in marriage*. Baltimore: Johns Hopkins University Press.

Spanier, G. B. (1983). Married and unmarried cohabitation in the United States: 1980. *Journal of Marriage and the Family 45*, 277-288.

Spanier, G. B., & Margolis, R. L. (1983). Marital separation and extramarital sexual behavior. *Journal of Sex Research 19*, 23-48.

Spreitzer, E., & Riley, L. E. (1974). Factors associated with singlehood. *Journal of Marriage and the Family 36*(3), 533-542.

Stafford, R., Backman, E., & di Bona, P. (1977). The division of labor among cohabiting and married couples. *Journal of Marriage and the Family 39*(1), 43-57.

Staples, R. (1981). Black singles in America. In P. J. Stein (Ed.), *Single life: Unmarried adults in social context*. New York: St. Martin's.

Starr, J., & Carns, D. (1972). Singles in the city. *Society 9*, 43-48.

Stein, P. (1983). Singlehood. In E. Macklin & R. H. Rubin (Eds.), *Contemporary families and alternative lifestyles*. Beverly Hills, CA: Sage.

Stein, P. J. (1975). Singlehood: An alternative to marriage. *Family Coordinator 24*(4), 489-503.

Stein, P. J. (Ed.). 1981. *Single life: Unmarried adults in social context*. New York: St. Martin's.

Stone, L. (1977). *The family, sex and marriage in England 1500-1800*. Harmondsworth, UK: Penguin Books.

Straus, R. (1976). Changing oneself: Seekers and the creative transformation of life experience. In J. Lofland (Ed.), *Doing social life*. New York: Wiley.

Straver, C. (1981). Unmarried couples: Different from marriage? *Alternative Lifestyles 4*, 43-74.

Streib, G. F., & Hilker, M. A. (1980). The cooperative "family": An alternative lifestyle for the elderly. *Alternative Lifestyles 3*(2), 167-184.

Stroebe, W., & Stroebe, M. (1986). Beyond marriage: The impact of partner loss or health. In R. Gilmour & S. Duck (Eds.), *The emerging field of personal relationships*. Hillside, NJ: Lawrence Erlbaum.

Sussmann, M. B. (1975). The four F's of variant family forms and marriage styles. *Family Coordinator 24*(4), 563-576.

Swain, D. (1978). Alternative families. In P. G. Koopman-Boyden (Ed.), *Families in New Zealand Society*. Wellington, NZ: Methuen.

Tanfer, K. (1987). Patterns of premarital cohabitation among never-married women in the United States. *Journal of Marriage and the Family 49*, 483-497.

Thompson, A. P. (1983). Extramarital sex: A review of the research literature. *Journal of Sex Research 19*(1), 1-22.

Thompson, A. P. (1984). Emotional and sexual components of extramarital relations. *Journal of Marriage and the Family 46*, 35-42.

Trost, J. (1981). Cohabitation in the Nordic Countries: From deviant phenomenon to social institution. *Alternative Lifestyles 4*, 401-427.

Van Ussel, J. (1977). *Life in communes* (In Dutch). Deventer: Van Loghum Slaterus.

Van Wijk, P. H., & Geist, C. S. (1984). Psychosocial development of heterosexual, bisexual and homosexual behavior. *Archives of Sexual Behavior 13*(6), 505-544.

Voeller, B., & Walters, J. (1978). Gay fathers. *The Family Coordinator 27*(2), 149-157.

Walshok, M. L. (1971). The emergence of middle class deviant subcultures: The case of swingers. *Social Problems 18*, 488-495.

Watson, M. A. (1981). Sexually open marriage: Three perspectives. *Alternative Lifestyles 4*, 3-12.

Watson, R. E. L. (1983). Premarital cohabitation vs. traditional courtship: Their effects on subsequent marital adjustment. *Family Relations 32*(1), 139-148.

Weeks, J. (1977). *Coming out: Homosexual politics in Britain, from the nineteenth century to the present,* London: Quartet Books.

Weggemans, T., Poldervaart, S., & Jansen, H. (Eds.) 1985. *Woongroepen: Individualiteit in groepsverband*. Utrecht: Het Spectrum.

Weis, D. L., & Jurich, I. (1985). Size of community of residence as a predictor of attitudes toward extramarital sexual relations. *Journal of Marriage and the Family 47*(1), 173-178.

Weiss, R. S. (1973). *Loneliness: The experience of emotional and social isolation*. Cambridge, MA: MIT Press.

Whitam, F. L., & Zent, M. (1984). A cross-cultural assessment of early cross-gender behavior and familiar factors in male homosexuality. *Archives of Sexual Behavior 13*(5), 427-439.

White, J. W. (1987). Premarital cohabitation and marital stability in Canada. *Journal of Marriage and the Family 49*, 641-647.

Whitehurst, R. N. (1969). Extramarital sex: Alienation or extension of normal behavior. In G. Neubeck (Ed.), *Extramarital relations*. Englewood Cliffs, NJ: Prentice-Hall.

Whitley, B. E. Jr. (1987). The relationship of sex-role orientation to heterosexuals' attitudes toward homosexuals. *Sex Roles 17*(1/2), 103-113.

Wiersma, G. E. (1983). *Cohabitation, alternative to marriage? A cross-national study.* Boston: Martinus Nijhoff.

Wolf, D. G. (1979). *The lesbian community.* Berkeley: University of California Press.

Yamaguchi, K., & Kandel, D. B. (1985). Dynamic relationships between premarital cohabitation and illicit drug use: An event-history analysis of role selection and role socialization. *American Sociological Review 50*(8), 530-546.

Yankelovich, D. (1974). *The new morality: Profile of American youth in the seventies.* New York: McGraw-Hill.

Yankelovich, D. (1982). *New rules. Searching for self-fulfillment in a world turned upside down.* New York: Bantam.

Yelsma, P. (1986). Marriage versus cohabitation: Couples' communication practices and satisfaction. *Journal of Communication 36*(4), 94-107.

Zablocki, B. D. (1980). *Alienation and charisma: A study of contemporary American communes.* New York: Macmillan.

About the Authors

Bram P. Buunk, Ph.D., is an Associate Professor in Psychology at the University of Nijmegen, the Netherlands. He received his Ph.D. from the University of Utrecht in 1980. Dr. Buunk has published over 80 scholarly articles and four books on topics such as inequity in marriage, jealousy, social comparison processes, marital communication, friendship and social support, and occupational stress. He has served on the boards of various professional organizations and scientific journals, including *Alternative Lifestyles, Journal of Social and Personal Relationships* and the *Review of Personality and Social Psychology*. Dr. Buunk has been a visiting lecturer at many American universities. In 1983–1984 he was a Fulbright Senior Scholar at the Department of Psychology of the University of California, Los Angeles.

Barry van Driel, M.A., is a graduate student in Social Psychology at the University of California, Santa Cruz, and a Doctoral Candidate in Sociology at the University of Nijmegen, the Netherlands. He has written several scholarly articles on the subject of the so-called new religious movements, focusing on the societal reaction to these largely communal groups. His main interests, in addition to variant lifestyle patterns, include social movements, deviance, mass media, social tolerance, and cross-cultural psychology.